Instructor

The LORD of PROMISES

by LeRoy Lawson

STANDARD PUBLISHING

Cincinnati, Ohio

39988

Scripture quotations are from the New International Version of the Bible, copyright 1978 by New York International Bible Society, used by permission.

Over 100,000 copies in print
Third printing: June, 1983

Library of Congress Cataloging in Publication Data:

Lawson, E. LeRoy.
  The Lord of promises.

  1. Jesus Christ—Words.   2. (Promise Christian theology)   I. Title.
BT306.L38 1983   226′.06   82-17034
ISBN 0-87239-611-8

INSTRUCTOR'S GUIDE

The writing of every book presents its own frustrations. The challenge in this one has been in trying to compress so many promises into thirteen short chapters. So much to say, so little space to say it in.

You may have the same problem as you prepare to teach. Every promise reminds you of another one, every Scripture studied will make you wonder why I did not include several others on the same subject, and every subject will seem too lightly developed. The fault is only partly mine. The publishing company must share the blame, because a publisher necessarily sets limits on the length of the book. Otherwise some writers—like this one—will go on indefinitely.

But the real culprit is Christ himself. The incredible promises of the Lord of the universe defy adequate exploration in a few pages or a brief class period. His vision is too grand, His wisdom is too profound, His challenge is too unsettling to allow us to feel adequate as author or teacher.

So do the best you can in the time you have, and trust the Spirit of God to help your students claim Jesus' promises as their own.

As you read the discussion questions for each chapter, you'll notice that many of them seem quite personal. You may wish to word some of them a little more tactfully than I have, but not too tactfully. Do not be too cautious in leading your students to think pretty seriously about Jesus' promises. They are no good, after all, unless they are believed, accepted, and acted on. Your purpose in teaching will be to lead your class members into a more positive Christian life, one animated by the joy, forgiveness, adventure, freedom, and other remarkable promises of Jesus.

You'll need to study the chapters in their entirety. Jesus doesn't make promises glibly. Each one is founded on truth to be lived, not just a wish to be hoped for. Adventure involves risk, joy demands love, love requires service, forgiveness expects forgiving, freedom insists on commitment. There is nothing cheap about Jesus' promises, so be certain that you lead your class to consider the cost as well as the blessing.

iii

As you prepare to teach, let me make some suggestions:

1. Read and reread each Scripture carefully, both the text for the lesson and the Scriptures quoted or cited in the chapter. Be confident that you understand these before facing your class. If you don't, they'll soon find you out.

2. Meditate on these Scriptures with thought and prayer. Ask God to open your mind *and* heart to their meaning. I am stressing both because your preparation is more than a mental exercise; it is also the yielding of your total self to the truth of God's Word.

3. Read the chapter through quickly, noting the major points. Then reread it slowly, underlining what seems important to you, writing notes in the margins, putting an exclamation point by something you agree with, a question mark or a bold NO where you think I'm wrong.

4. React to the chapter honestly. Do not make the mistake of attempting to teach what you cannot believe. Do not hesitate to argue with me as you teach the lesson to your class, but be certain that you can offer the students a satisfactory explanation of your position. You don't have to agree with me—but you don't want to disagree with Scripture.

5. React to it devotionally, also. Use this study as an opportunity to check your own reliance upon Jesus' promises. Do you really believe Him? Do you act as if you do? Can you openly tell others about what the Lord has done for you? Do you know from personal experience that He keeps His promises—because you have trusted Him and found Him faithful?

6. Now look at the brief notes for the assigned chapter. It will be helpful to memorize the key verses so you will have no doubt of the central focus of the lesson. You don't need to memorize the lesson theme, of course, but keep it in mind as you read and as you teach so that you do not stray too far from the subject.

The questions are designed to get you started. You'll add others that I have not listed. As you add to the list, however, try to be certain that they are relevant to the promise under discussion. It's very easy to lose control of the classroom through an ill-worded question.

Now you are ready. The Lord of Promises will help you as you help others to know Him better.

iv

A WORD ABOUT THE FOLLOWING CHAPTERS

The Lord of Promises is designed for your personal as well as group study. You may wish to study all thirteen chapters of this book, as it forms a three-month series for Sunday school or home Bible groups.

If you are using it as part of Standard Publishing Company's Vacation Bible School program, you will want to select either five or ten chapters, depending upon the length of your school. For five sessions, chapters 2, 5, 7, 8, and 10 are suggested; for ten sessions, chapters 2 through 11.

I. HE PROMISES FREEDOM

John 8:31, 32

Key verse: "Then you will know the truth, and the truth will set you free." John 8:32

Lesson theme: In a few words Jesus outlines the steps to personal freedom.
   A. Belief leads to discipleship.
   B. Discipleship leads to truth.
   C. Truth leads to freedom.

DISCUSSION QUESTIONS:
1. In what ways have *you* found new freedom since becoming a Christian?
2. Americans like to boast that we belong to a free country. Do we? Are we really free?
3. Do you believe *that* Jesus is the Christ or *in* Jesus Christ? What's the difference?
4. What does it mean to be a *disciple* of Christ?
5. What do you mean when you say you belong to this church?
6. Why does Jesus equate holding to His teaching with being His disciple?
7. How can knowing the truth set us free?
8. Why does the author insist that "only the disciplined person is prepared to recognize the truth when he sees it"?

9. Does Jesus promise absolute freedom? If not, what is the freedom He promises?

II. HE PROMISES
THAT YOU CAN BE BORN AGAIN

John 3:1-21

Key verse: "Unless a man is born again, he cannot see the kingdom of God." John 3:3 (or use John 3:16)

Lesson theme: God has us surrounded: Father, Son, and Holy Spirit are one in the business of rescuing lost persons and breathing new life into them. Therefore: you *can* be born again.

DISCUSSION QUESTIONS:
1. What do *you* think? Is it possible for a mature adult to be really changed?
2. Jesus says we must be born of water and Spirit. To what does the *water* refer? What is the role of the *Spirit*?
3. In what way does Jesus' example of the bronze snake *differ* from His own cross?
4. Why didn't God choose Sechele's method of converting people?
5. What could we know about God if we did not know Jesus?
6. In your own words, describe the love of God.
7. Since God has us surrounded, how can we keep from being saved?

III. HE PROMISES
THE JOY OF ABIDING LOVE

John 15:1-17

Key verse: "I have told you this so that my joy may be in you and that your joy may be complete." John 15:11 (or use John 15:10)

Lesson theme: Jesus tells us how to experience the joy of abiding love.
   A. "Remain in me and I will remain in you."
   B. "Bear much fruit."
   C. "Love each other as I have loved you."

DISCUSSION QUESTIONS:
   1. How would you distinguish joy from happiness?
   2. What is the source of joy?
   3. What does the author mean in this sentence: "You have to work harder when your source of strength is in the air rather than in the vine"?
   4. If Jesus is dependent upon us to bear fruit for Him, what should we be doing?
   5. Is it actually possible for a person to be a lifelong Christian and still be a withering branch? How can we keep ourselves from withering?
   6. How can we guard against becoming hypocrites?
   7. Why is joy impossible apart from love?
   8. Who has complete joy?

IV. HE PROMISES TO MAKE US MORE THAN ORDINARY HUMAN BEINGS

John 13:1-17

Key verse: "No servant is greater than his master." John 13:16

Lesson theme: Jesus shows the way to become more than an ordinary person.
   A. He demonstrates: "I have set you an example."
   B. He teaches: "No servant is greater than his master."
   C. He promises: "You will be blessed if you do them."

DISCUSSION QUESTIONS:
1. Wouldn't you have called Napoleon a more-than-ordinary human being? Do you agree with Beethoven's outrage?
2. Why does Jesus insist (in Luke 22:24-27) that we must not be like Gentile rulers? What is wrong with them?
3. Why did Jesus prefer the way of humility? Why do we hesitate to follow Him?
4. Where did you come from? Where are you going? What differences do your answers to these two questions make?
5. The author says, "The secret of humility is a strong self-image." Do you agree?
6. Can you suggest other blessings that come from following Jesus' example?
7. Which of the blessings discussed has meant the most to you?

V. HE PROMISES FORGIVENESS

Luke 15:11-32

Key verse: "There is more rejoicing in heaven over one sinner who repents than over ninety-nine righteous persons who do not need to repent." Luke 15:7

Lesson theme: Jesus promises forgiveness like that which the father freely grants his son in this famous parable.
Note the following:
A. The unworthy son.
B. The eager father.
C. The self-righteous elder brother.
D. The justice of society; the mercy of God.

DISCUSSION QUESTIONS:
1. Why didn't the son just give up and die among the pigs? What keeps us going when we are desperate?

2. Why didn't the father "bash him"? Is it possible that the boy "put it over on the old man again"?
3. Why do we find it so hard to forgive and to believe in God's forgiveness?
4. Could society run on the ethics of the father?
5. Why is forgiveness an essential ingredient in friendship?
6. What do we mean when we say that forgiveness forgets?
7. What does the cross of Jesus have to do with the theme of this lesson?

VI. HE PROMISES EVERLASTING LIFE

John 11

Key verse: "I am the resurrection and the life. He who believes in me will live, even though he dies." John 11:25

Lesson theme: Jesus summarizes the Christian's hope in death.
  A. Life and resurrection are found in Jesus.
  B. I will never die, even though I die.
  C. I will live while I live.

DISCUSSION QUESTIONS:
1. Do you like the farmer's sermon on the honeybee's stinger? How would you describe the Christian's view of death?
2. Why do you suppose Jesus' closest friends and disciples could not comprehend His power over death?
3. If we believe in life after death as much as we say we do, why are we afraid to die?
4. Read 1 Corinthians 15 for Paul's description of the resurrection body. What do you think he means?
5. What difference does belief in life after death make on our lives this side of death?
6. If you were told you would die at midnight tomorrow night, what difference would it make in your next twenty-four hours?

VII. HE PROMISES A SURPRISING LIFE

John 12:20-28

Key verse: "The man who loves his life will lose it, while the man who hates his life in this world will keep it for eternal life." John 12:25

Lesson theme: The route to real life is surprising.
  A. You get by giving.
  B. You live by dying.
  C. You succeed by serving.

DISCUSSION QUESTIONS:
  1. Do you agree with Huxley that "a man's worst difficulties begin when he is able to do as he likes"?
  2. What is the secret of Paul's contentment?
  3. What is the secret of success in any field?
  4. What does the author mean, "You do not get by wishing, but by giving"?
  5. Could you say with Jones, "Well, I don't have to live. I can always die"? What does he really mean?
  6. Does Jesus' teaching here work in the world of hard knocks? Could you apply it, for example, to business or family life?
  7. What has been your finest hour? Were you thinking of yourself or others?
  8. Have you been surprised by what you have received in your service for the Lord?

VIII. HE PROMISES A POWERFUL LIFE

John 14:8-14

Key verse: "Anyone who has faith in me will do what I have been doing. He will do even greater things than these, because I am going to the Father." John 14:12

Lesson theme: Jesus challenges us to demonstrate far more power than we have thought possible for us.
  A. The statement: "Anyone who has faith in me will do what I have been doing."
  B. The promise: "He will do even greater things than these because I am going to the Father."

DISCUSSION QUESTIONS:
  1. Do you believe Jesus means what He is saying? Why, then, haven't we done more?
  2. In what respect can we be Jesus' successors?
  3. What does the author mean by this statement: "As He was a missionary from God to us, so we are missionaries from Christ to the world"? What should we do, then?
  4. What does it mean to be "in Christ"?
  5. Do you agree with Shoemaker that "God is more eager that we should have spiritual power than we are to possess it"? If so, how should we appropriate more of His power?
  6. What should your church do to demonstrate the powerful life Jesus promised?

IX. HE PROMISES ANSWERED PRAYER

John 14:13, 14

Key verse: "And I will do whatever you ask in my name, so that the Son may bring glory to the Father." John 14:13

Lesson theme: Jesus promises answered prayer.
- A. The purpose of prayer.
- B. The possibilities in prayer.

DISCUSSION QUESTIONS:
1. Share your experiences of answered prayer with the group.
2. Have you had any disappointments in prayer? Perhaps you would like to share these, too.
3. Does Jesus' promise mean that He will grant our every wish?
4. What is the purpose of prayer?
5. The author says, "I am better for His answers than for my requests." Are you?
6. What does asking in His name mean?
7. What can God *not* give us when we pray?
8. What is the risk involved in praying?

X. HE PROMISES AN ADVENTUROUS LIFE

Matthew 28:16-20

Key verse: "Therefore go and make disciples of all nations, baptizing them in the name of the Father and of the Son and of the Holy Spirit. . . . And surely I will be with you always." Matthew 28:19, 20

Lesson theme: Obeying Christ's commission leads to an adventurous life.

A. Adventurous living begins with Christ's orders.

B. Early Christians led adventurous lives.

C. Adventurous Christians still obey His orders—and enjoy His promises.

DISCUSSION QUESTIONS:

1. How can you "leave home spiritually"?
2. What is the secret of zestful living?
3. Does Jesus mean *you* in the Great Commission?
4. How are *you* responding to the Commission?
5. Has your life been as exciting as you would like? Has the study of this chapter given you some ideas of how to put more adventure into your living?
6. What does it mean to "smilingly wash one's hands of the consequences" of obedience to Christ?
7. Hammerskjold linked service with freedom from fear. Was he right?
8. What difference does your "religion" make in your character?
9. If you could live your life again as you have lived it this time, would you?

XI. HE PROMISES
A PEACEFUL LIFE

John 14:27; Romans 5:1-11

Key verse: "Peace I leave with you; my peace I give you. I do not give to you as the world gives. Do not let your hearts be troubled and do not be afraid." John 14:27

Lesson theme: Only Jesus, whose ways are not the world's ways, can give you peace.
A. Peace in time of trouble.
B. Peace with God.

DISCUSSION QUESTIONS:
1. What would happen to Dagwood if each of his days were like the one described in this chapter? What would happen to you?
2. Can our defense department guarantee peace for our country?
3. What is the effect of neighbors' protecting themselves with guns?
4. What was the source of Paul's peace in Acts 27?
5. Why *not* try God?
6. Look carefully at the contrast in Romans 5. On which side are you? What difference has it made?
7. How do you "relax" into God?
8. Is it possible to live without anxiety about anything?

XII. HE PROMISES
A SPIRIT-FILLED LIFE

John 14:15-18, 25, 26; 16:12-15;
Acts 2:38

Key verse: "Repent and be baptized, every one of you, in the name of Jesus Christ so that your sins may be forgiven. And you will receive the gift of the Holy Spirit." Acts 2:38

Lesson theme: Jesus promises that the Holy Spirit will help us meet His expectations.
  A. The Holy Spirit points to Christ.
  B. The Holy Spirit builds up the church—and helps us to do our parts.
  C. The Holy Spirit helps the Christian know and live the truth.

DISCUSSION QUESTIONS:
  1. Why does the Christian life seem too hard sometimes?
  2. Why does the Spirit seek to bring glory to Christ and not to himself?
  3. What's wrong with a religion of excitement?
  4. What do you think is the most important gift of the Spirit? Why? What does the Bible say about their relative importance?
  5. Are you talented or gifted? What's the difference?
  6. Is yours an honest church? A mission-minded church? A united church? Would you call these characteristics of a spiritual church?
  7. What do you expect the Holy Spirit to do for you?
  8. Read and discuss the work of the Spirit in Galatians 5:16-23.

XIII. HE PROMISES
A CONSEQUENTIAL LIFE

Matthew 25

Key verse: "Then they will go away to eternal punishment, but the righteous to eternal life." Matthew 25:46

Lesson theme: When you die, you will get what you have prepared for.
  A. Consequences in time.
  B. Consequences in eternity.

DISCUSSION QUESTIONS:
   1. Do you think this chapter belongs in a book on the promises of Jesus?
   2. Do you agree that you are as valuable as Matthew 25 says you are? What difference will your answer make in the way you live?
   3. Have you lived long enough yet to see the consequences of your life on others? Are you pleased with the results?
   4. Why can't a person do whatever he wants to?
   5. Should you bother God with your problems?
   6. Would you like for the way you are now living to go on forever?
   7. Is it hard to get ready for Heaven?
   8. Why is it important to memorize John 3:16 *and* 17?
   9. Matthew 25 speaks of carelessness (1-13), excusemaking (14-30), and lack of compassion (31-46) as obstacles on the pathway to Heaven. Does any of these standards of judgment surprise you? How do you think you would be measured?

The LORD of PROMISES

by LeRoy Lawson

 STANDARD PUBLISHING

Cincinnati, Ohio

39989

Scripture quotations are from the New International Version of the Bible, copyright 1978 by New York International Bible Society, used by permission.

Over 100,000 copies in print
Third printing: June, 1983

ISBN 0-87239-612-6

Copyright © 1983, The STANDARD PUBLISHING Company, Cincinnati, Ohio.
A Division of STANDEX INTERNATIONAL Corporation. Printed in U.S.A.

"For no matter how many promises God has made, they are 'Yes' in Christ."

2 Corinthians 1:20

PREFACE

I can't get the horrible story out of my mind. I've heard it several times. As much as I want to say it could never have happened, I'm certain it did. It is about a man who loved his son dearly, but maimed him for life because of his misguided attempt to toughen him against the hurts which life inflicts on all of us. One thing he wanted the boy to understand above all else: he must trust nobody. Nobody.

So when he came home one evening and his son bounded down the stairs to greet him, he stopped the boy abruptly on the landing. He reminded him once more that people are not to be trusted. Ever.

"Yes, Daddy."

"You can't trust anybody, can you?"

"No, Daddy."

"But you can trust Daddy, can't you?"

"Oh, yes, Daddy."

His Daddy then held out his arms and told the boy to jump, which is what the boy had been waiting for. But when he jumped, his father stepped aside and let him fall with a crash to the floor.

"You see," he said to his son, "You must trust nobody."

This father's attitude is exactly what this book is *not* about. *The Lord of Promises* introduces the Person whom it is possible for us to trust completely.

The misguided father was partially correct to warn his son. Some people are not worthy of a child's trust. But there must be somebody, somewhere, the boy can trust. Without faith in someone, fear will devour him, anxiety will paralyze him. He must not trust indiscriminately, of course. His father could have taught him the wisdom of believing only in those who keep their promises. Only the proved faithfulness of the promiser is worthy of the believer's trust.

That is why the God who invites us to believe in Him knew He must first prove himself dependable. The Bible is a record of the promises He has made to His people and His faithfulness in keeping them. We are surrounded by a host of witnesses of God's faithfulness, the author of Hebrews tells us, including such greats as Abel, Noah, Abraham, Moses, Gideon,

Barak, Samson, Jephthah, David, Samuel, and the prophets. In each case these heroes acted out their belief in God's promises. Through faith they conquered kingdoms, administered justice, shut the mouths of lions, quenched the fury of the flames, and escaped the edge of the sword. They are giants of faith—they *trusted* the Lord of Promises.

This, then, is the order: first promises, then faith, then life.

"His divine power has given us everything we need for life. . . . He has given us his very great and precious promises, so that through them you may participate in the divine nature and escape the corruption in the world caused by evil desires" (2 Peter 1:3, 4).

In this book we will be exploring some of the many magnificent promises Jesus makes to His disciples, promises which add up to "the promise of life that is in Christ Jesus" (2 Timothy 1:1). We gladly follow Him because whenever we have tested Him, we have found He keeps His word. Unlike the cruel father who trusted nobody, Jesus never steps aside to let us fall. So we still sing the song we learned years ago in Sunday school.

"Standing on the promises *I cannot fall,*
Listening every moment to the Spirit's call,
Resting in my Savior as my all in all—
Standing on the promises of God."

Jesus has promised—so we trust Him.

Because we trust Him, we obey Him.

As we obey Him, we become more like Him.

Since we are more like Him than like the princes of this world, we seem different from the rest of humanity.

We *seem* different because we *are* different. We are not anxious; we are not frightened; we are not easily bullied into conformity with this world.

We are being transformed—by the Lord of Promises.

CONTENTS

HE PROMISES FREEDOM

John 8:31, 32

We begin with the promise of freedom. The subject has been on my mind since my first television appearance, an event that took place in my college years.

Of course, by then I was already an experienced radio actor, having appeared as Tiny Tim in Dickens' *Christmas Carol* when my fourth grade class presented the classic over local station KTIL in Tillamook. In spite of my experience, however, I was pretty nervous when some other students and I went before the TV cameras to speak on the values of a Christian college education. It was a double challenge: to make a reasonable case for my college while fighting off an irresistible urge to flee from the studio.

I'll always be grateful for the opportunity, though, since it forced me to evaluate my education as I had never done before. It made me aware of the freedom I enjoyed as a Christian student. Because of my faith in Christ, "the way, the *truth,* and the life," I realized I had been free to explore any subject under any professor without fear. He had freed my mind to explore His whole universe because all truth is His.

Academic freedom is only one dimension of the liberty we enjoy in Christ, but at that stage in my education, when many of my fellow students and no few professors sneered at all Christian students as intellectually inferior and bound by prejudice, it was exciting to discover how free I really was. I later attended a college in which a philosophy professor was reputed to have boasted that no student could graduate from there and still believe in God. I had my own boast, which was that as a Christian, I could attend any college, study any subject, and learn from any professor without being afraid of what I might be exposed to because I had already discipled myself to the One who had revealed the highest truth to man.

Since those undergraduate days, John 8:31, 32 have been among my favorite verses. In these few words Jesus almost casually outlines the Christian path to personal freedom.

BELIEF LEADS TO DISCIPLESHIP
The first step to personal freedom is to become Jesus' dis-

ciple. "If you hold to my teaching, you are really my disciples," Jesus tells the Jews who had believed Him. He appeals for faith that is more than a belief *that* but is belief *in.* I can tell you that I believe *that* my father lives. This expresses one kind of faith. But when I tell you I believe *in* my father, I have another kind of faith in mind. I believe *that* the United States of America is a great country; but when I tell you I believe *in* the U.S.A., I imply a loyalty and commitment that involves my whole being. If I believe *that* you are a fine person, you will thank me for the compliment; if I assure you I really believe *in* you, you will know that you can always count on me to support you. The belief Jesus wants us to have in Him is this second kind, the kind that "holds on" to His teaching, that leads to discipleship.

The apostle Paul uses a stronger word than *disciples* to speak of the same act of commitment. His word is *servant* or *slave.* He has become the servant of Christ—and the servant of no other. As a servant he obeys his Master's will, holds on to his Master's teaching, and follows Him as a disciple follows his teacher.

At a recent convention I picked up a nineteenth century book by a frontier preacher, the *Autobiography of Elder Samuel Rogers.* As I read his account of frontier preaching, one episode in this traveling evangelist's career captured my attention. He was riding through an area of Pennsylvania containing many beautiful natural springs. He approached one of them just as a fine silver-mounted carriage halted and a servant stepped out, holding a silver pitcher and cup. Rogers asked him for a drink, but the servant replied, "If you please, sir, when I have served my master." And, after serving his master, he returned to give Rogers a drink. The preacher mused over what had just happened.

> "Here was one, bought with his master's money, who was more faithful and understood his obligations better than we who have been bought with our Master's blood."

He was so impressed he adopted as his own motto, "My Master first; then, others."

"If you hold to my teaching" *first,* in spite of every distraction, every appeal for your allegiance, then "you are really my disciples." Jesus appeals for a new understanding of faith: our faith is not something that belongs to us, but something we belong to. That language is helpful: You ask me what church *I belong to* and I tell you that *I belong to* the Christian church. When I use these words in other contexts, they mean ownership. My stereo set *belongs to* me, my house *belongs to* me. In a slightly different sense, even my children belong to me. When I say, then, that *I belong to* my church, I am suggesting that I am responsible to the church, under the control of the church, under the Lordship of the church's Head. My religion is not a fad, a game to play or a pastime to indulge myself in when nothing more pressing keeps me from it. If I truly belong to the church and the church's Lord, He controls me! I am a disciple.

DISCIPLESHIP LEADS TO TRUTH

"Then you will know the truth. . . ." First there must be discipleship, which means disciplined learning. Just as my faith cannot be casual, neither can my studies be casual. A disciple of Jesus is one who disciplines himself to learn from Jesus all the truth that Jesus has to teach him.

Jesus' call for discipleship implies that truth is not easy to attain. Not long ago a friend of mine clipped a page from the *Wall Street Journal* which he thought I'd enjoy. I did because it contains several quips that illustrate how hard it is to know the truth—about anything. Here are some of them:

> —"If polls are so accurate, why are there so many polling companies?"
> —"A man with one watch knows what time it is; a man with two watches is never sure."
> —"Good judgment comes from experience; experience comes from bad judgment."
> —"Education is the process of moving from cocksure ignorance to thoughtful uncertainty."

Taken together, they mean that a little humility will go a long way in our pursuit of truth. Humility as a student of life is precisely the characteristic Jesus demands. You cannot be a disciple—a student—without it. We would be wise to borrow this ancient prayer and make it our own:

> From the cowardice that shrinks from new truth,
> From the laziness that is content with half-truths,
> From the arrogance that thinks it knows all truth,
> O God of Truth, deliver us.

Jesus' assignment from His Father was to lead us into the truth. Our assignment from the Son is to follow Him into the truth. "The Word became flesh and lived for a while among us . . . full of grace and truth" (John 1:14). But not everyone accepted Him. Even His own people rejected Him. Their greatest teachers had taught them to sing,

"Show me your ways, O Lord, teach me your paths; guide me in your truth and teach me. . . ."
"Send forth your light and your truth, let them guide me . . ." (Psalm 25:4, 5; 43:3).

But when their desire was granted and the Truth came to guide them, many preferred their half-truths to the full revelation in Christ. In the record of Jesus' rejection by His own people, we learn the sad fact that truth is not revealed to just anybody, but only to those who seek it. That is why discipleship must come first. Only the disciplined person is prepared to recognize the truth—or the lie—when he sees it. Hitler boasted that "through propaganda you can make people believe that Hell is Heaven and Heaven is Hell." Yes, you can make some—perhaps most—people believe propaganda, but you will not fool those who have a divine measure for separating fact from fiction.

Hitler's success forces us to ask ourselves: How do we know when we are hearing propaganda? By what standard do we judge what we hear? Let me get specific: How do you judge our country's foreign policy? Is it based on truth or propaganda? How do you judge television commercials? Do you believe them? How do you know when your elected officials are lying and when they are not? How do you prepare your children to know when they are hearing the truth from their schoolteachers and when they are not? For that matter, how do you teach them to know when *you* are telling the truth?

Is there such a thing as truth? Has it been spoken? By whom? Can it be lived? If so, are you living it?

Your answers to these questions affect everything about your life. Some circles laugh at the very idea that someone has brought the truth to us and that we can choose to accept or reject it. In a college course in personality theory, for example, the professor (whose knowledge of rats was greater than his knowledge of people) asked his class whether science's growing knowledge of human behavior would soon enable us to predict individual and group behavior. More than 50 students agreed.

One student objected. "I don't think that the human personality can be completely measured by the scientific method," he said. He argued that in spite of the many powerful influences upon an individual, there is still in him a "spark of freedom" which enables him to choose his own way in spite of these influences. He would not ever be totally predictable. There was a moment of dead silence, finally broken by a man in the back of the room who called out, "That sounds like a religious idea to me." He spoke it scornfully, but the speaker accepted it as a compliment. It was—it is—a religious idea. It is Christ's idea. It enabled the speaker to resist the unfounded assumptions of his psychology class. That student was experiencing the freedom I discovered as a Christian student; he had a standard by which to measure the professor's theory.

What Christ teaches is vital to our fullest development. He teaches that you can be free to become; you don't have to remain what you are. You are more than the sum of the forces—be they psychological, economic, social, or whatever—that have played upon you in the past. You can be free.

But you must pay the price of freedom.

It was Jesus, after all, who taught His disciples that they could not be His disciples if they would not take up their crosses and follow Him. He insisted that they were not worthy of Him if they loved their lives more than they loved Him. He warned them that whoever would save his life would lose it and that only one willing to lose his life for His sake (the Truth's sake) would save it.

TRUTH LEADS TO FREEDOM

". . . And the truth shall set you free." Not just free from whatever it is that I don't like. Christ's freedom is not the aimless rebelliousness of the 1960s, but more the freedom of America's founding fathers. They rebelled all right, but after they had won their independence from Britain, their real struggle for freedom began. Then they learned with what grueling hard work freedom is preserved and self-government maintained. As Niebuhr has so wisely stated it, "Man is most free in the discovery that he is not free."

That is why the apostle Paul, the great preacher of freedom in Christ, never promised absolute freedom. There is no such thing. Paul found his fullest freedom in his slavery to Christ. By pledging his allegiance to Jesus Christ, whom he would serve at whatever cost, he was free from anyone else. He would never have to bow his knee to priest or politician or money or monarch. He could obey God alone. He would, therefore, heed the voice of his Lord and no other. "It is for freedom that Christ has set us free. Stand firm, then, and do not let yourselves be burdened again by a yoke of slavery" (Galatians 5:1).

My ministry has been motivated to a large extent by gratitude to God for my freedom. Jesus has set me free to become myself, to think for myself in His Spirit, to love without restraint those whom He has taught me to love, to choose whom and what causes I will serve. He has also taught me, in the words of Eric Hoffer, that "the basic test of freedom is perhaps less in what we are free to do than in what we are free not to do." I am free to live a life-style not dictated by Madison Avenue or even by the Joneses. I am free to abstain from the social habits that dominate polite society. I don't have to drink what others drink, smoke what they smoke, buy what they buy, think what they think, cheat as they cheat, lie as they lie, or struggle to succeed as they struggle to succeed. Not that I am free from guilt in all these matters (I am still subject to a slave mentality from time to time), but I don't *have* to do any of them. Christ has set me free.

Do you remember *The Odyssey* from your school days? Homer's great epic of Odysseus' return from the Trojan wars includes the episode in which he has to sail his men closely by the island of the sirens, seductive creatures with bodies of birds, heads of women, and voices of angels. With their incredibly beautiful singing they can so enchant sailors that they rush their ships toward the island to hear more of the lovely music, only to be dashed to their death on the dangerous rocks. Odysseus knows the extreme danger they are in, so he devises a plan to get them safely past the temptation. He will plug the ears of his sailors so they cannot hear and will have them lash him to a mast so tightly he cannot move.

14

It is an acceptable plan, but somebody has a better idea. Aboard ship is a man named Orpheus, the greatest harp player in the world. His music surpasses even the singing of the sirens. Orpheus plays for Odysseus and his men as they sail by the island, and his more beautiful music sets them free from the seductions of the sirens.

We are surrounded by a host of sirens, all tempting us to come to them, to accept their thoughts and customs as our own. So we rush toward first this one and then that one, only to dash our lives upon the dangerous shores. It is impossible to block out their insinuating music; impossible, that is, except by overcoming it with the even more enchanting music of the Singer of Truth. Those who listen to Him and *hold on* to His songs will know He sings the Truth. By that truth, He will set them free.

HE PROMISES
THAT YOU CAN BE BORN AGAIN

John 3:1-21

By the time you have reached my age, you've just about given up. Your youthful dreams have faded, your high ideals have corroded, and your ambitions have adjusted themselves to your limited abilities. You'd like another chance at making something of yourself, but you don't really believe that chance will come your way. With moral and spiritual blemishes that match your physical ones, you concentrate on surviving to old age with as few hardships as possible.

Nicodemus is not the only person who ever doubted that one can be born again. He speaks for every generation of middle-aged disappointments that has ever lived. He is convinced that he cannot start over.

Jesus insists he can. In fact, he must!

Undoubtedly, Nicodemus is more than a little nervous as he pays his secret visit to Jesus. He is a member of the Jewish ruling council, the highest honor granted an orthodox Jew. He is a recognized leader of his people. If his colleagues in the Sanhedrin find out he has consulted this uncertified teacher, they will raise some embarrassing questions, to say the least.

Nicodemus is puzzled, however, and wants to learn more of this man. He cannot deny the power Jesus has displayed in His miracles, power attributable only to God. Yet Jesus' teachings violate the strict traditional teachings of the Jews. How can this paradox be resolved? Can Jesus really be from God? If so, what should Nicodemus do about His teachings? He cannot follow Him and at the same time uphold the traditions of the Jewish elders. He must hear Jesus further.

As John records the conversation, Jesus indulges in no small talk. He plunges right into the core of His surprising teaching: "Unless a man is born again, he cannot see the kingdom of God." No minor adjustments of religious traditions will make them right; the most fervent application of their teachings cannot save a person. Jesus requires nothing less than radical rebirth. This new start cannot be accom-

16

plished through adding some new rules to old, nor transfer-
ring allegiance from one rabbi to another, nor even by moving
from non-church membership to membership. Only new birth
will suffice.

THE ROLE OF THE HOLY SPIRIT

The words translated "born again" can also be "born from
above." They imply that a rebirth experience is not something
over which a person has full control. He can provide the water, as in Christian baptism, but he cannot control the Spirit.

When Jesus says Nicodemus must be born of water,
Nicodemus probably thinks of the familiar proselyte baptism,
in which a non-Jew can wash away his "Gentileness" in the
process of adopting Judaism as his faith; or he may think of
John the Baptist, the famous prophet who has been practic-
ing a baptism of repentance in the Jordan River. Nicodemus
understands the meaning of these baptisms and the repentance they call for. But when Jesus couples water with Spirit,
He introduces the mystery of God's initiative in rebirth and
leaves Nicodemus bewildered.

Only the Spirit can give birth to a new spirit in a person. And
the Spirit "blows wherever it pleases"; it does not take orders
from us. Bible specialists may categorize, systematize, and
dogmatize about the Spirit to their hearts' content, but He
"blows wherever it pleases" Him.

It was God's Spirit who gave us life:
> "And the Lord God formed man from the dust of the
> ground and breathed into his nostrils the *breath* of life,
> and man became a living being" (Genesis 2:7).
> *Breath* is the word we translate *Spirit.*

We cannot live without the Spirit:
> "If it were his [God's] intention and he withdrew his *spirit*
> and *breath,* all mankind would perish together and man
> would return to the dust" (Job 34:14, 15).

As natural life is attributed to God's giving spirit (or breath)
to man, so eternal life is associated with God's giving of His
Holy Spirit to man. Flesh is flesh—strictly human, natural. But
even flesh is dependent upon God, just as spirit is dependent
upon Spirit. Jesus is drawing a distinction between the strictly
natural human being and the newly reborn spiritual being
within the human form. While we cannot ever understand all

17

we would like to know about the Spirit, we can see the effects of His power in the reborn life. We "hear its sound."

Having grown up on the Oregon coast, I appreciate Jesus' comparison of Spirit with wind. You cannot see, but you can hear and feel, the powerful "Sou'westers" that drive against the coast, overpowering and bending and shaping the trees at will. In this manner, you cannot see the Spirit, Jesus says, but you can discern the effects of His shaping power in the life of the reborn Christian. Every person whose life has been caught up by this unseen power can testify to the exciting adventures and unexpected shaping he has enjoyed in the Lord.

THE ROLE OF THE SON

Jesus leads Nicodemus from the Spirit, whom he cannot see, to the Son, whom he can see and because of whose work he can be born anew.

Establishing His authority ("We speak of what we know. . . . No one has ever gone into Heaven except the one who came from Heaven—the Son of Man"), Jesus then turns Nicodemus' attention from the initiative of the Holy Spirit to the objective, redeeming act of the Son on the cross. The Spirit moves, the Son sacrifices, and the observer believes in order to have life.

To help His struggling student grasp the Son's role in redemption, Jesus reminds him of the familiar story of Moses and the serpent (see Numbers 21). God had sent snakes among the Israelites in order to quiet their incessant grumbling against Moses and himself. The snakes did their job and the people quickly repented. "We sinned when we spoke against the Lord and against you. Pray that the Lord will take the snakes away from us" (v. 7). So Moses prayed and God had him fashion a bronze snake and hang it on a pole. When the people would look upon it, they would live.

The snake served two purposes: to remind the people of God's punishment for their complaints and to save those who believed enough to look on it. The people were saved through their suffering, repenting, and believing. But here Jesus departs from His Old Testament example. Salvation *now* comes through the Son's suffering, not the people's.

But he was pierced for our transgressions, he was

18

crushed for our iniquities; the punishment that brought us peace was upon him, and by his wounds we are healed (Isaiah 53:5, 6). He himself bore our sins in his body on the tree, so that we might die to sins and live for righteousness; by his wounds you have been healed (1 Peter 2:24).

David Livingstone's first convert at Chonuane, in what was then the Belgian Congo, was Chief Sechele. The new Christian made rapid progress in his ability to read the Bible, especially enjoying the book of Isaiah. "He was a fine man, that Isaiah," Sechele said. "He knew how to speak." As zealous to convert his people as he was to grow himself, the chief chastized Livingstone for his slow methods of evangelism. "Do you imagine these people will ever believe by your merely talking to them? I can make them do nothing except by thrashing them, and if you like, I shall call my head-man and with our litupa (whips of rhinoceros hide) we will soon make them all believe together."[1]

Sechele's is just the method God deliberately did not choose. Instead, He lifted up another Healer, this time His own Son, to make it possible once and for all for men and women to have eternal life. The Spirit can encourage them, the Son can die for them, but the people must believe in the God who cares enough to go to this extremity to save them.

"You can believe what I am telling you, Nicodemus, because no one has ever gone into Heaven except the Son who came from Heaven—the Son of man. I have been there; I know what I am talking about. I know why the Son of Man must be lifted up—to make it possible for you to attain eternal life. More than this, I have been offered up by my Father himself so that you will know how much He loves you. I have come to show you His love."

What promise is in these words! And what despair if He is not believed. In his play, *The Devil and the Good Lord,* twentieth-century French atheist Jean-Paul Sartre portrays the increasing disillusionment of Goetz, a soldier who converts to belief in God—but then wonders where God is. He prays; he demands a sign; he gets no reply. Finally, he concludes that God is nothing but the emptiness over his head, the gap in the door, the hole in the ground. "Silence is God. Absence is God. God is the loneliness of man."[2]

If only he had looked at Jesus.

Without Jesus, what can we know of God? Without the cross, what can we believe about God? When we meet the Son of Man, we begin to comprehend something about God and something about ourselves.

Bishop Pickett, who ministered for years in India, tells of Angrahit, a convert to Christ who turned to the Lord initially to find salvation from his poverty and oppression as a member of one of India's lowest castes. He said he found what he was looking for. He used to be hungry most of the time. When God saved him, He took him away from his drinking and gambling, which made it possible for him to get food for his family.

> "God has forgiven my sins," he said, "taken away my fear, removed my superstition, and given me faith and hope and purpose. If I could not have known Jesus before I understood his salvation, I could never have known him, for it was by knowing him that understanding came."[3]

That is what Jesus is talking about. The Son of Man must be lifted up so that people can believe in Him. Their belief in Him leads to further understanding, and their understanding to a transformed life.

The Spirit and the Son cooperate to encourage the belief that leads to new birth and eternal life.

THE ROLE OF THE FATHER

All this is from God. It was God who so loved the world that He gave His one and only Son. It was God who did not want anyone to perish but to have eternal life. It was God who did not send His Son into the world to condemn the world, but to save the world through Him. God the Creator has become God the Father, who loves all His children and does not want to lose one of them.

A few years ago, at a national convention, I watched something like the love of God in action. Myron Taylor, a superb preacher, was delivering one of his typically powerful sermons, but I confess I wasn't paying very close attention. I was distracted by a beautiful little girl, hardly more than a year old, barely able to walk and trying to master the steps just down the aisle from me. She was a delicate, fair blonde in a pink dress resplendent with frills, freshly starched and pressed for this special occasion. She was not doing her dress any favor with her crawling, but she didn't care. She was too busy climbing, falling, and climbing again to worry about anything else. Just a few feet away, not interfering but never taking his protective eyes off her, was her father, obviously enjoying her happiness but intent that she not hurt herself. The father was guarding his newly-born one who had so much to learn, loving yet permitting her the freedom to grow.

That is the love of God. He grants us new birth through the Spirit, made possible through His Son, and still presides over us in the hope that we shall do nothing to cause ourselves to perish.

Yet many perish because they do not know the love of God. *New Yorker* magazine published a cartoon many years ago depicting a solitary straggler in a vast desert. He has managed to crawl up to a large billboard poster of what at first appears to be a map. In the lower right-hand corner is an X. Above it are printed the words, "You are here." There is nothing else on the board.

There is our problem. Dying in a godless wasteland, we seek rescue. We crawl to psychologists or sociologists or journalists or physicians or academicians. They all point to the X. "Here is where you are," they say. They don't know how to help us further. They say, "No one has ever gone into Heaven. . . ." Then they stop. They will not finish the sentence, "except the one who came from Heaven—the Son of Man." They leave us in this out-of-joint world to drink deeply of its bitter springs, hoping that somewhere we can find pure water, but we find none. So the suicide rate keeps climbing, alcoholism proliferates, the illicit drug trade booms, and hope gives way to despair.

But we cannot blame our world for all that is amiss in our lives. At the root, we know the problem. Like Pogo, we have met the enemy, and "he is us."

So I must pray:
> "Dear God,
> I have a problem!
> It's me.

And I hear God answer me:
> Dear Child,
> I have an answer!
> It's ME."[4]

Nicodemus hears this answer. He hears that the Holy Spirit is like a wind blown from God to make it possible for a person's spirit to be reborn from above.

He hears that Jesus will have to be lifted up on a cross so that everyone can look at Him and see the love of God revealed and know that this is how much God wants to save whoever believes.

He hears that the promise of rebirth took shape in the heart of God, who wants more than anything else to say to every hurting person on earth: "Dear Child, I have an answer for your problem. It's me."

He hears that God has us surrounded: Father, Son, and Holy Spirit are one in the business of rescuing lost persons and breathing new life into them.

This is your promise: you *can* be born again.

NOTES

[1]George Seaver, *David Livingstone: His Life and Letters.* New York: Harper & Brothers, 1957, p. 97.

[2]Jean-Paul Sartre, *The Devil and the Good Lord,* trans. Kitty Black. New York: Vintage Books, 1960, pp. 140-141.

[3]J. Waskom Pickett, *The Dynamics of Church Growth.* Nashville: Abingdon Press, 1963, pp. 38-39.

[4]*Christian Reader,* May/June 1977, p. 15.

HE PROMISES
THE JOY OF ABIDING LOVE

John 15:1-17

"What makes you so happy?"

"It's a good morning," I answered without thinking. To tell the truth, I was so surprised by the stewardess' question I had no ready answer.

Until that moment I hadn't been aware I was happy.

I was enroute from Cincinnati to Phoenix after speaking for a writers clinic. Breakfast was over, and I was reading and meditating a little while, savoring my second cup of coffee. I still don't know what signals the stewardess was reading when she interrupted my reverie.

She was right, though. I was happy—more than happy, I was joyful. If there is one good reason among the many others that could be given as *my* reason for being a Christian, it is found in Jesus' words in John 15: "I have told you this so that my joy may be in you and that your joy may be complete." Joy is an experience so pervasive that you are often unconscious of it. When you are filled with the love, variety, color, challenge, excitement, usefulness, and adventure that are the natural results of life in the Lord, you don't have time to take your psychic pulse to find whether you are joyful or not. You just are. You abide in Christ, and He abides in you, and that's all there is to it.

Well, *almost* all there is. Christian joy is a continuing sense of well-being that derives from Christ's promise to keep you in His love. His love is always available, but we may not always be aware of being held by His love. Such awareness does not come automatically to every believer but to those who are confident that He will not let them go.

In this passage Jesus explains what His disciples must do to experience the complete joy (verse 11) He promises with His abiding love.

"REMAIN IN ME, AND I WILL REMAIN IN YOU"

Live close to the source of life, in harmony with the Lord, as a vine is in harmony with its branch. Abiding with Christ is as

23

necessary for real life as bread ("I am the bread of life") and water ("whoever drinks the water I give him will never thirst"), as necessary as a branch's dependence on its vine.

If God is indeed our Creator and Sustainer, it naturally follows that a person is at his best when he is being constantly nourished by remaining close to the Creator. This obvious truth is so frequently ignored, however, that people are surprised to discover what a difference returning to God can make in someone.

Norman Vincent Peale tells in one of his books of a man who came up to talk to him following his message for a convention of the Association of Radio and Television Broadcasters. The man told Dr. Peale of a fellow worker at the local radio station who had been in conflict with everybody—his wife, his associates at work, himself. The managers would have fired him if he had not been an old and valued hand. Their patience was running thin, however, when for some reason they decided to place him in charge of religious programming. It was a strange decision, since the worker was in no way a religious man. He had to sit in the studio week after week as the religious programs were being piped out to the homes in their radio audience. He hated having to listen, but it was his job.

"Then we saw something happening to him," Dr. Peale's informant told him. It was as if God had penetrated the bitter worker's consciousness through the programs. His fellow workers saw him lose his bitterness and become a harmonious personality. He became a happy person and an efficient worker again. No one should have been surprised. He was merely returning to his source, finding joy in his experience of God's love.

This complete joy cannot be purchased at the counter nor put on with the latest fashions, in the manner of the insecure woman someone described as being vogue on the outside but vague on the inside. She has all the appearance of prosperity but is undefined and out of tune with herself.

She resembles the woman staring out of a full page advertisement in the *Chicago Daily News* a few years back. With a smile she invited readers to subscribe to the magazine she was promoting. Part of her pitch read, "Maybe I won't ever wear a wig, but if wigs are becoming fashionable, I'd like to be told now. I want to be able to talk about things that really count these days."

If you are not living in harmony with God, then you feel driven to meet the demands of your society, living in a fashionable neighborhood, driving the finest automobiles, and working two jobs in order to purchase all the important things which airwaves and newsprint insist are necessary to feed and adorn the body. You have to work harder when your source of strength is in the air rather than in the vine.

I cannot help contrasting the woman's concern for wigs with the total lack of interest in fashion which some Christians express. I am thinking particularly of some very close friends who had been missionaries in Africa before returning to America to assume an executive role in missions. They are two of the calmest, fullest, most joyful persons I have known. Of course, you would never ask them how wigs are doing these days. They seem unfashionably uninterested in the latest clothes fads, or the most popular cars, or where to find the best neighborhoods. And when you are with this couple, you somehow can't introduce such subjects. Instead, you talk about God; you share your stories of the joys of the ministry; you cry a little over the needs of the world. When you leave them, you feel renewed, as if the spiritual juice of the true vine were flowing within your veins. There is nothing vague about their faith; their nourishment comes from the Spirit within, not from status symbols without. If they haven't viewed the latest movie or attended the symphony or kept up on the National League race, you don't condemn them for being out of vogue. Instead, you marvel that they have made you sensitive to what is infinitely more important.

They force you to ask just how important it is to keep up to date. I remember being shocked in graduate school when a professor snorted that he only read the newspaper when he could find nothing important to do. Twenty years later I am beginning to identify with his values. I am even questioning this age of electronic magic. Have our computers and video recorders and word processors and stereophonic equipment made any of us more complete persons? Sir Arthur Sullivan's prediction has come true. In 1883, Thomas Alva Edison played his new invention, the phonograph, for Sullivan. Later, he wrote the inventor a little note: "I'm astonished and somewhat terrified at the result of this evening's experiment—astonished at the wonderful power you have developed and terrified at the thought that so much hideous and bad music may be put on record forever!" He was right to worry.

"Remain in me," Jesus pleads. "Stay as close as a branch to its vine, and I will remain in you"—"that your joy may be complete."

"BEAR MUCH FRUIT"

Jesus' second requirement has to do with being good for something. Live effectively . . . matter to somebody . . . participate in God's work . . . bear fruit. The branches are dependent on the vine; that fact we have established. But the vine also depends on the branches to bear the fruit. The vine can live, but it can never accomplish its purpose without the branches. Jesus' analogy is a simple reminder that the Lord has made us partners in His work. He has limited himself to allow us the privilege of being conduits for His love.

"Remain in me, and I will remain in you. No branch can bear fruit by itself; it must remain in the vine. Neither can you bear fruit unless you remain in me."

The King James Version's *abide* is a stronger word than *remain,* connoting intimacy, comfortableness, and absence of stress or tension in our fellowship with the Lord. *Abiding* certainly is not to be identified with the frenzied organized activities that are often called "church work." Young Christians should be cautioned against trying to prove their quality as born-again believers by the quantity of their activities.

Karl Jung, the famous psychoanalyst, tells of a church leader whose disposition began to sour when he was forty; by the time he was fifty-five it had curdled. A bitter, cynical, thoroughly disagreeable man by then, he made it plain to all his acquaintances that the Spirit of Christ did not abide in him. Still, he kept up his church activities out of a sense of duty instead of devotion. Then one night he sat bold upright in bed and said to his startled wife, "Now, at last I've got it. As a matter of fact, I'm just a plain rascal." He then harmonized his life, but not by drawing closer to the Lord. He abandoned himself to his rascality in riotous living. In the end he was good for nothing. He had become honest, but lost. In the earlier years he had gone through the motions of religion but did not allow God's love to flow through him. He bore no fruit; he found no joy.[1]

His is an extreme, but not unheard of, case. At the other extreme are faithful Christians who are just as useless, though sweeter-spirited. They devote themselves to prayer, Scripture reading, and many acts of personal piety, but their spiritual pursuits are inward. Concerned about their own salvation, they fail to reach out to others in Christ's name. They desire to abide in Christ's love, but they are not concerned about being effective for others. Jesus warned that they are like branches that are cut off because they are withering. Whereas our rascal went through the external motions of effective Christian living with an empty soul, these Christians strive to fill their souls to the exclusion of bearing fruit in the lives of others. In both cases, outer conflicts with inner life.

Jesus insists that we live without hypocrisy, that we *be* what we *seem.* His church needs no spiritual schizophrenics and no more play actors. God's work depends on effective Christians.

E. Ray Jones explains this better than I can. In one of his church papers he writes of Cecil Samara, a sold-out fan of the University of Oklahoma football team. In leaving instructions for his funeral, Mr. Samara requested to be embalmed with his forefinger pointing in the fashion of a football fan shouting, "We're Number One." His casket would be red and white, the university's colors. He would be buried in his red and white suit. Donations in his name would go to the U of O scholarship fund.

Not too long before making his funeral arrangements, Samara had a dentist prepare a new set of upper teeth, with a red letter set in six of them, spelling out Big Red. He wanted even his smile to reflect his team loyalty. He dressed in red and white cowboy boots, a red leather belt, a red-faced watch and red and white glasses and hat. He was a man unashamed to demonstrate his inner convictions in his external behavior.

You would not have had to ask Cecil Samara what he believed.[2] There is no hypocrisy here.

I am not proposing that we go and do likewise, exactly. What Jesus has in mind can more appropriately be illustrated by Zaccheus, the pocket-lining tax collector who became a follower of the Lord. "Look, Lord!" he told Jesus when he accepted Him as his master. "Here and now I give half of my possessions to the poor, and if I have cheated anybody out of anything, I will pay back four times the amount." His new belief required different behavior. By bringing his business practices in line with his internal convictions, he could live in harmony with his Lord and become an effective disciple, bearing the kind of fruit that the vine wished to produce—and his joy would be complete.

"LOVE EACH OTHER AS I HAVE LOVED YOU"

Jesus' third requirement is inseparable from the other two. To bring yourself into harmony with God, and to harmonize your external and internal conduct so that you can effectively bear God-designed fruit, you have to love the other branches on the vine. "My command is this: Love each other as I have loved you." You cannot be one of Christ's and hold yourself aloof from other disciples, as Jesus makes so uncomfortably plain in His great commandment (Mark 12:28-34; Matthew 22:33-40).

A long time ago *Saturday Evening Post* published a cartoon depicting a man staring into his mirror. He had probably just crawled out of bed and stumbled to the wash basin. There he is, staring at bloodshot eyes and stubble of beard, bags bulging under his eyes, talking to himself. "You're all I've got," he says. Wouldn't it be frightening to be in his mirror, having no one else to love? Or to be one of the deluded who think they can find the best in life by looking out for themselves only? They discover that in the end, they are all they've got.

Jesus' hope is that our joy may be complete—an impossibility without love. And love is only love when it expresses itself toward others. The individual who shuts himself up in his little world to do his own thing or be his own person finds, in time, that life has turned against him, like a boomerang that has missed its target.

Like the boomerang, which only returns to its thrower if it has failed its mission, a person's life is also designed to hit a target ("I chose you to go and bear fruit"). When the life fails, it returns to itself in a distorted form. Preoccupied with what *he* thinks, what *he* feels, what *he* wants, what *he* has to have, the selfish person misses joy completely. "My command is

28

this," Jesus says—and if you disobey Him in this matter, you cannot have joy—"Love each other *as I have loved you.*" As John says, "We have passed from death to life, because we love our brothers" (1 John 3:14). The opposite is true, also. Without loving, we pass out of life into death. Life boomerangs.

Who has complete joy? Let me tell you of a beloved old rabbi, so holy that his students thought when he disappeared periodically he must be going up to Heaven to see God. One day as he left them, a student secretly followed to see where he went. He trailed him to a cottage where his teacher changed out of his rabbinical robes into coarse peasant clothes. In the cottage was an invalid woman whom the rabbi served, preparing her food, cleaning her hovel, making her comfortable.

The student returned to his fellows, who asked him, "Did the rabbi ascend to Heaven?"

"Yes," he replied, "if not higher."[3] He had found the secret of his rabbi's joy.

The three commandments for abiding in Jesus' love, then, are these:

"Remain in me, and I will remain in you."

"Bear much fruit."

"Love each other as I have loved you." Do them, and your joy will be complete.

NOTES

[1]*Modern Man in Search of a Soul.* New York: Harcourt, Brace and World, Inc., 1933, p. 105.

[2]"Minister Muses." *Clearwater Christian,* January 21, 1976.

[3]From "If Not Higher" by Isaac Loeb Peretz. Qouted by Stephen M. Panko, *Martin Buber. Waco: Word Books, 1976, p. 23.*

HE PROMISES TO MAKE US MORE THAN ORDINARY HUMAN BEINGS

John 13:1-17

At first Beethoven admired Napoleon. When the little but mighty general seized Paris and reconstituted the government of France in 1799-1800, Beethoven praised him for bringing order to the chaos of the Revolution. He compared him with the greatest consuls of ancient Rome and dedicated his newest symphony to him, writing Buonaparte at the top of the title page, and at the bottom, his signature, LUIGI VAN BEETHOVEN.

Beethoven forcefully deleted the dedication, however, when word was brought to him that First Consul Bonaparte had just declared himself Emperor. He flew into a rage, crying out, "Is then he, too, nothing more than an ordinary human being? Now he will trample on all the rights of man, and indulge only his ambition. He will exalt himself above all others, become a tyrant." He tore the title page in two. Then, taking another sheet, he gave his composition a new title, "Sinfonia eroica," by which it has been known ever since.[1]

Beethoven did not hold the ambitious general in awe. He admired Napoleon, the great restorer of order to France, but he despised the self-serving, ambitious, tyrannical ruler Napoleon became. Beethoven had hoped this general would be different; he was disillusioned to find out that he was nothing more than an ordinary human being with very ordinary drives.

He discovered what Jesus had cautioned against centuries earlier. Even on their last evening together, while He inwardly agonized over His coming betrayal and death, He had to settle a dispute about who among His disciples was the greatest. They were behaving, Jesus scolded them, not like disciples of the Lord, but like petty Gentile kings who lord it over their subjects.

"You are not to be like that. Instead, the greatest among you should be like the youngest, and the one who rules like the one who serves. For who is greater, the one who is at the table or the one who serves? Is it not the one who is at the table? But I am among you as one who serves" (Luke 22:24-27).

Jesus refused to treat himself as a common king. He was different; He had deliberately chosen the servant role. And He expected the same from His disciples. He told them, in effect, "I don't want you to be ordinary persons. You must be different. I have washed your feet to show you in what way you must be different."

"I HAVE SET YOU AN EXAMPLE"

The disciples should not have been surprised when Jesus assumed the role of the lowest servant in the household, stripping off His outer garment, wrapping a towel around His waist, and washing their feet. It was unheard of for an ordinary teacher to humble himself in this fashion before his students, to be certain, but Jesus was no ordinary teacher. He had been teaching lessons of humility since His birth. A more modest beginning could not be imagined: no place in any inn for His parents, a manger for a birthplace, a flight to Egypt like common refugees, a carpenter's shop for His schoolhouse. His ministry developed the same theme: abasing himself before the prophet John in the baptismal waters of the Jordan, being rejected by the leaders of His nation, existing by freewill gifts and the hospitality of friends, accumulating no savings, and having nothing material to show for His services.

"Foxes have holes and birds of the air have nests, but the Son of Man has no place to lay his head," he said (Matthew 8:20).

Then came His final act of humiliation, the cross. He was dragged like a common criminal through Jerusalem's crowded streets, insulted in the rigged court trial, and ridiculed through a mock coronation with its crown of thorns, robe of purple, and streams of spittle down His face. Then the spikes, the vinegar and bile, and the greatest humiliation of all: "He saved others; He can't save himself."

From beginning to end Jesus exemplified humility. We prefer not to follow. He appeals to us to imitate Him, promising blessings for the meek. But it is hard to answer His appeal, even for the most religious among us.

A few years ago I spent several days in Las Vegas. While

31

there, I was surprised to see a fleet of English doubledecker buses, apparently retired from active duty in Britain's cities. I learned that the buses had been purchased by a large church in the city and were used as a rather brilliant advertising gimmick in a town that is immune to anything less flamboyant. My admiration abated quickly, however, when I saw that each bus flourished a large photo of the pastor. I could no longer be certain who was being promoted, the church or the man.

I thought of John the Baptist, that charismatic personality calling people to repentance out in the Jordan valley. Such great crowds he attracted, such a hold he had on his audience! He could have persuaded them to follow him anywhere. Instead, he warned them against thinking too highly of him:

"After me will come one who is more powerful than I, whose sandals I am not fit to carry" (Matthew 3:11).

John never forgot that God called him to *prepare* the way for the Christ, not to *be* the Christ. "I am not the Christ," he told his followers, "but am sent ahead of him. . . . *He must become greater; I must become less*" (John 3:28-30). John thought himself unworthy to carry Jesus' sandals. He would not have hesitated to wash His feet.

Ralph Waldo Emerson tells of a young convent nun who claimed to have some rare gifts of inspiration and prophecy. Her abbess advised the pope of her wonderful powers. To test the young woman's claims, the pope sent a trusted counselor, known later as St. Philip Neri, to interview her. Philip left in haste, traveling by mule over muddy roads and, upon arriving, took no time to change his spattered clothes. Instead, he asked the abbess to send the nun immediately. When she came in, Philip asked her to draw off his dirty boots. The young lady had become accustomed to more deferential treatment because of her fame. She drew back in anger and refused to help him. Philip thereupon abruptly concluded the interview, ran from the convent, mounted his mule and returned instantly to the pope, to whom he reported, "Give yourself no uneasiness, Holy Father, any longer: here is no miracle, for here is no humility."[2] She was just an ordinary human being.

"NO SERVANT IS GREATER THAN HIS MASTER"

Whether we like it or not, if we would call Jesus Lord, we

must follow Him in service. It is one thing for us to go to a prayer meeting for Jesus, but quite another to clean boots. We will praise the Lord—if we are also praised.

In the poets' corner in London's famed Westminster Abbey, you can find this memorial to John Milton. That is, it was intended to be a memorial to the Puritan poet, but someone else steals the show:

In the Year of our Lord Jesus Christ
One thousand seven hundred thirty and seven
This Bust
of the Author of PARADISE LOST
was placed here by William Benson, Esquire
One of the two Auditors of the Imprest
to his Majesty King George the Second
formerly
Surveyor General of the Works
to his Majesty King George the First.
Rysbrack
was the Statuary who cut it.

In this inscription the servant looms larger than the master. Milton is an excuse to exalt Benson (with Rysbrack getting in on the act). In a later day he would have advertised his talents on a double-decker bus!

Among the most ludicrous cases of self-advertising I have read comes this one from the sixteenth century, when Ottoman power was at its height and all Europe seemed about to fall before it. Suleiman the Magnificent wrote a letter to the king of France, identifying himself as the writer of the epistle in these few words:

I who am the Sultan of Sultans, the Sovereign of Sovereigns, the distributor of crowns to the monarchs of the surface of the globe, the shadow of God on earth, the Sultan and Padishah of the White Sea, the Black Sea, Rumelia, Anatolia, Caramania, Rum, Sulkadr, Diarbekr, Kurdustan, Azerbaijan, Persia, Damascus, Aleppo, Cairo, Mecca, Medina, Jerusalem, all Arabia, Yemen and other countries which my noble ancestors (may God brighten their tombs) conquered and which my august majesty has likewise conquered with my flaming sword, Sultan Sulayman Khan.[3]

The man was somewhat impressed with his importance,

wouldn't you say? We can only laugh at his arrogance. He is so ordinary!

He is like Mr. Cunningham, in an episode on television's *Happy Days,* fretting that he might not be elected as the Grand Poopah of his Leopard Lodge. Unfortunately, the ambition to be Grand Poopah afflicts every generation and every tribe. It seems especially fatal in Washington, D.C. Harry Truman was musing to Merle Miller one day about the many politicians he had watched fall into trouble there because they began thinking they were pretty special.

> It's very easy to do that in Washington, and I've seen it happen to a lot of fellas. But I did my best not to let it happen to me. I tried never to forget who I was and where I'd come from and where I was going back to.[4]

Truman has exposed the secret of humility: never forget who you are, where you came from, and where you will return to. His words closely paraphrase John's description of Jesus as He takes up towel and basin:

> Jesus knew that the Father had put all things under his power, and that he had come from God and was returning to God; so he got up from the meal, took off his outer clothing, and wrapped a towel around his waist. . . .

Because Jesus knew who He was, He did not consider it demeaning to serve His disciples. He was His Father's Son; He had come from God and would be returning to God. He had experienced the glory of Heaven itself, so what could any earthly title or privilege mean to Him? He did not need to protect His self-image. He was not ordinary.

The secret of humility is a strong self-image. The strong person can be gentle, the important person can listen to a child, the spiritually secure person can tolerate the less secure. If you know who you are—a child of the King, a servant of the Lord—you need no flattery to keep your spirits up. You have been called by the extraordinary Lord to be a more than ordinary person.

"YOU WILL BE BLESSED IF YOU DO THEM"

Few blessings are to be found in the usual pursuit of praise or power. Jesus would have agreed with Shakespeare:

> 'Tis better to be lowly born,
> And range with humble livers in content,

Than to be perk'd up in a glistering grief,
And wear a golden sorrow.[5]

Richard Armour does not say it as elegantly, but he says it right:

Now that I'm almost up the ladder
I should, no doubt, be feeling gladder.
It is quite fine, the view and such,
If just it didn't shake so much.[6]

The blessings Jesus has in mind are better than the top-of-the-ladder variety. Let me suggest some of them:

1) *Closer fellowship with the Lord.* Peter is horrified when the Master offers to wash his feet. That simply is not done! Peter will not permit it.

"Unless I wash you, you have no part with me," Jesus answers. Peter has to learn that he does not always know what is best. The Master has reasons of His own, reasons in tune with eternity's values and not with any culture's distastes. So long as Peter feels compelled to advise and judge his Lord, there can be no real fellowship between them.

2) *Closer fellowship with other disciples.* "You also should wash one another's feet," Jesus instructs them. Genuine fellowship is sharing; quite literally, it could be washing each other's feet. More significantly, it is learning to put the needs and honor of another before your own. Someone has said that in Heaven everyone will be bowing to everyone else. If so, I think the bow will be followed by an embrace. To serve another is to come to love another.

3) *Deeper thoughtfulness.* Albert Schweitzer rightly said that "the deepest thinking is humble." Humility is open to new knowledge. Arrogance believes the flattery with which it is so easily manipulated, humility is not fooled by flattery. An over-enthusiastic lady once asked Winston Churchill if it did not thrill him that his speeches always brought overflow audiences. "It is quite flattering," he told her, "but whenever I feel this way, I always remember that if instead of making a political speech I was being hanged, the crowd would be twice as big."[7]

4) *A quiet dignity.* "There is no humiliation for humility," someone counseled me. But pride does indeed go before a fall. When John Wesley was walking along one of London's narrow sidewalks one day, he encountered a stranger who

35

refused to step aside for him to pass. The stranger remarked that he would not get out of the way of a fool. Mr. Wesley, not offended in the least, replied quietly, "I will," and stepped around him. The man who boasts that he would be the first to admit his faults if he had any is the target of every jester around. But the person who can pray with the publican, "Lord, have mercy on me, a sinner," never has to fear that he will be humiliated. He has already knelt before the Lord, who lifts up the humble. (See Psalm 147:6; Proverbs 16:5; Psalm 149:4, 25:9; Proverbs 11:2.)

The human race has granted no more honor to anyone than to Jesus of Nazareth. He gained His reputation not by arrogating power to himself,

> but [He] made himself nothing,
>> taking the very nature of a servant,
>> being made in human likeness.
> And being found in appearance as a man,
>> he humbled himself
>> and became obedient to death—
>> even death on a cross!

(Philippians 2:7, 8)

You know what God did for Him. Since then, no one has been able to think of Jesus as an ordinary human being.

He invites us likewise to forsake the ordinary.

NOTES

[1]Will and Ariel Durant, *The Age of Napoleon.* New York: Simon and Schuster, 1975, p. 575.

[2]*Essays and English Traits,* "The Harvard Classics," ed. Charles W. Eliot. New York: P. F. Collier & Son, 1909, p. 298.

[3]Quoted by H. Richard Niebuhr, "Illusions of Power." *The Pulpit,* April, 1962.

[4]*Plain Speaking,* an oral biography of Harry S. Truman by Merle Miller. New York: Berkley Publishing Company, 1973, 1974, p. 10.

[5]*King Henry VIII,* II, iii.

[6]Quoted in Dr. Laurence J. Peter, *The Peter Prescription.* Bantam Edition, 1973, p. 137.

[7]Kay Halle, *Irrepressible Churchill.* New York: World Publishing Co., 1966.

HE PROMISES FORGIVENESS

Luke 15:11-32

There is something incurable about parenthood. How else do you explain the prodigal son's father? His son had impertinently demanded his inheritance while his father was still living. Then, with the worst possible judgment, he squandered everything his father had given him in wine, women, and song, dissipating himself and disgracing his family name. With no thought of tomorrow, he saved nothing; when the famine hit, he became desperate. He took the only job he could get, the lowest, vilest one a member of his race could imagine. He became a feeder of pigs.

How long it took for the young man to come to his senses Jesus does not say, but when he did, he turned toward home. He was disgusted with himself. His clothes were foul, his food was wretched, the stench of his body was repulsive. The keeper of the pigs had become one of them. He starved with a hunger that was more than physical.

He had sinned. No excuses, no rationalizations could erase his guilt. "I have sinned against heaven and against you," was all he could say to his father.

He could easily have succumbed to despair and died there among the swine. Or he could have taken up permanent residence on skid row in any city, among other lost souls who believe there is no way back for them. He could have believed with Omar Khayyam that

> The moving Finger writes; and having writ,
> Moves on: nor all your Piety nor Wit
> Shall lure it back to cancel half a line,
> Nor all your Tears wash out a Word of it.

This young man did not despair, however, because his memory of his father gave him hope. His father had not willingly given him his inheritance; he had warned him what might happen in the far country. He had tried to protect the boy from himself, but to no avail. When a young man has made up his mind to leave his father's love, there's no stopping him. So his father let him go, yet something in the way he said good-bye left open the door for the son's return. It would be worth it to try to return, anyway.

37

Maybe his father would not want him back as a son. He couldn't blame him. If not a son, then perhaps he could be his father's hired hand. Even that would be a promotion.

What he must have thought as he eagerly, yet hesitantly, made his way homeward. Would he be welcomed or rejected? Had his father been hurt too deeply to embrace him again? Would he want him anywhere near?

An equally anxious young man was homeward bound on a train. He confessed to his seatmate that he was a convict returning from prison to the parents he had shamed. While he was serving his time, he received no visits or letters from them; they were uneducated and very poor, reasons he hoped explained their lack of contact with him. Their silence made him unsure of their forgiveness.

He had tried to make it easy on them by writing ahead to say that if he was welcome, they should tie a white ribbon on the big apple tree near the tracks. If there wasn't one there, he would stay on the train, and they would not be embarrassed by him anymore.

As the train drew near his hometown, he lost his nerve. He couldn't look. His friend offered to watch for the tree for him, so they changed places. In just a few minutes, with his hand on the young convict's shoulder, the friend whispered emotionally, "It's all right. The whole tree is white with ribbons."[1]

He had been forgiven.

So had the prodigal. It was pure celebration—no penance required, no scolding delivered, no probation period set down. Nothing mattered more than this, that the son who was dead to his father had come alive again.

William Barclay tells of a Sunday school teacher who was studying this story with a class of slum children in Scotland. At this point in the story she asked, "What do you think his father did to him when he got home?" From the back of the class came an immediate answer, "Bash him!"[2] The little guy hadn't experienced this strange thing called forgiveness, so he could not expect the father would knowingly accept his son. Neither could another boy who heard a moving presentation of this welcome. "So," he exclaimed, "he put it over on the old man again!"[3]

They failed to grasp the tenacity of a father's love, just as Jesus' critics failed to comprehend the love of God, whom the father portrays in the parable. The Old Testament teaches that the Lord is "a forgiving God, gracious and compassionate, slow to anger and abounding in love" (Nehemiah 9:17), but the teachers of the law easily forgot this element in God's personality. They did not realize that Jesus was living out God's forgiveness in their midst. Later, when they would hear Him pray on the cross, "Father, forgive them, for they do not know what they are doing" (Luke 23:34), they would still fail to hear the voice of a forgiving God speaking through Him.

In this regard, the Pharisees and teachers of the law are our spiritual ancestors. We find it difficult to follow Jesus in His generous distribution of God's grace. We pray as He taught us, "Forgive us our debts," because we are desperate to have our obligations wiped away, but we mumble through the next part, "as we also have forgiven our debtors," hoping the Lord won't take us literally. Unfortunately for us, Jesus' very next word (Matthew 6:14, 15) proves that He does indeed mean it:

> "For if you forgive men when they sin against you, your heavenly Father will also forgive you. But if you do not forgive men their sins, your Father will not forgive your sins."

Jesus must have stressed the importance of this lesson many times, because Peter later raised the issue again: "Lord, how many times shall I forgive my brother when he sins against me? Up to seven times?" Peter was generous for a person brought up on the ethic of eye for eye and tooth for tooth. He must have been astounded to hear Jesus say, "Not seven times, but seventy-seven times (or seventy times seven)" (Matthew 18:22).

Such extravagant grace demands an explanation. Jesus provides it in the form of another story, this one about an unmerciful servant (see Matthew 18:21-35). His point is that the debt we owe God for forgiving our sins is so much greater than any debt owed us that we have no choice but to forgive others. Jesus promises no forgiveness "unless you forgive your brother from your heart."

The eternal wisdom of Jesus' teaching becomes obvious when we consider the alternative. Forgiveness breaks the chain of eye for eye, tooth for tooth. You never really get even in a cycle of retaliation; you just keep fueling the battle. The futility of repaying evil for evil was graphically pointed out by Winston Churchill, who was present in a meeting in which a speaker developed the theme that the ethic of retaliation was the only way to survive in this world. After he finished speaking, Chuchill finished him by asking, "Did you ever try to sting a bee?"

A decision to wreak vengeance assumes that I do not deserve to suffer. When I get even, I act as if I am an innocent person, which, of course, I am not. If someone has lied about me, I need to remember the little untruths I have told and got away with. If someone is jealous of me and does me an injustice, he reminds me that I have occasionally been tempted to covet and act unfairly. When a person begins to be honest, his honesty frequently retards his program for reforming his neighbors. It dampens his urge to get even. He forgives because he has been forgiven much.

I am not suggesting that this honesty is typical. Unfortunately vengeance is the more normal course. The attitude of ex-Prime Minister Zulkifar Ali Bhutto of Pakistan is far more typical. In prison, after being overthrown in office, Bhutto smuggled a note out of his confinement which threatened that "my sons will not be my sons if they do not drink the blood of those who shed my blood."[4] In that spirit Israelis drink the blood of Syrians, who drink the blood of Iraqis, who drink the blood of Egyptians, and so on and on it goes. The famous feud of the Hatfields and the McCoys only plays out in small what is pursued in large in international wars. Koreans hate Japanese, who hate Chinese, who hate Russians, who hate Americans. And for any sleight, war.

The villain in the parable is the elder son, vicious in his self-righteousness, ready to turn his repentant younger brother out again, like the Pharisees and teachers of the law, whose mutterings against Jesus prompted this parable. "Forgive us our virtues," Nietzsche has written. "God, I thank you that I am not like all other men—robbers, evildoers, adulterers—or even like this tax collector," prayed the Pharisee in Jesus' parable of the Pharisee and the tax collector (see Luke 18:9-14). He was as good a man as the elder brother, and just as hateful.

The ethics of the elder brother govern society. Justice, not mercy, is our demand—except for ourselves. A young man named Joe Turner is one of thousands who have learned this fact the hard way. He was out carousing one night with his buddies in Birmingham, Alabama. Next day he was arrested for a robbery he says he did not commit, but he was black, and then it was the fifties. He had no lawyer. After being forced to sign a confession, he says, he was sent to a prison road gang. He served four years of his sentence; then one day he escaped in the rain.

He ran away to Chicago, where he went to work, married, fathered children—and tried to forget. The personnel manager in his factory called him a "wonderful guy," remarking that he had been there for thirteen years and had never given even the slightest problem.

Joe was afraid he would be caught some day, and he was. Twenty years after he ran away he was taken into custody. In the meantime, he had lived an upright, decent, responsible life, taking care of his wife and children and paying his debt to society.

When they arrested him, Joe asked for mercy. But law is based on a policy of punishment for misdeeds; law does not operate on mercy. He was returned to jail. There was no forgiveness.

The desire for justice rules on a personal level, also. Two lifelong friends were also partners in a manufacturing business. Their families were close, with the daughter of one engaged to be married to the son of the other. Everything changed one day, though, when one of the partners secretly made a deal to join a competing firm. The betrayed partner, who had earlier indignantly rejected the same offer, vowed his revenge and risked his own bankruptcy in his determination to drive his former partner out of business. The deserter retaliated in turn, using his political influence to raise his former partner's property assessment. The son and daughter broke their engagement.

At this point the betrayed man's wife intervened. She pointed out that her husband had been the stronger of the two men in resisting the temptation to desert. Then, having proved himself strong, he was now proving himself weak by trying to take revenge.

She prompted her husband to invite the other family over so they could make peace. They did, and the two men became friends again, though they remained business rivals. And they are grandfathers of the same child. Forgiveness had broken the cycle of vengeance.

Only forgiveness can. We're talking about genuine forgiveness, by the way, the forgive and forget kind. We must not be like the wife who had just quarrelled with her husband. "Come now," he said to her, "I thought you had agreed to forgive and forget."

She replied, "Sure, but I don't want you to forget that I have forgiven and forgotten."

Real forgiveness forgets. It believes that healing the relationship is more important than harboring a grudge. It is strong enough to say "I'm sorry" even when it feels the other party should apologize first.

That is why the cross looms so large in the Christian faith. In order to break the cycle of retaliation, God sent His Son and let wicked humanity commit every injustice against Him. We beat Him, scourged Him, mocked and spat upon Him, killed and buried Him. And God said—"I forgive. I will not seek the blood of those who shed the blood of my Son. I will forgive those who ask, restore those who wish to be restored, adopt as My own children those who will accept My mercy. I will not get even."

The cycle of an eye for an eye, a tooth for a tooth, a bomb for a bomb, blood for blood has been broken.

He promises forgiveness.

NOTES

[1]Charles R. Hembree, *Fruits of the Spirit*. Grand Rapids: Baker Book House, 1969, p. 17.

[2]*The Mind of St. Paul*. New York: Harper and Brothers, 1958, p. 78.

[3]Harry Emerson Fosdick, *The Living of These Days*. New York: Harper and Brothers, 1956, p. 71.

[4]*Time,* February 19, 1979, p. 43.

HE PROMISES
EVERLASTING LIFE

John 11

"The news isn't good. I have cancer."

I didn't know much about cancer of the bladder when Van told me the results of his tests. He was in such fine emotional control that *my* shocked reaction dismayed *him.* He refused to let me express even momentary grief.

Only later did I learn the details. A slow-growing form of cancer, Van's illness had been developing for years with no apparent symptoms. When the first sign appeared, a little blood in the urine, it was too late. The best his doctor could promise was one to three years. Surgery was scheduled.

Lester Van Dyke is one of God's special servants. When he received this news, he was a robust, cheerful sixty-five-year-old who appeared at least ten years younger. "I've done it all," he would frequently tell his friends with a combination of regret and rejoicing. For years he had embarrassed himself and his family with uncontrolled bouts of drinking, even as he led an otherwise respectable life as a bank manager and community leader. He would later always identify himself as an alcoholic, never an ex-alcoholic, even though he had been sober for more than twenty years.

Sober regarding drink, that is, but never sober otherwise. From the moment of his conversion to Christ, he was a God-intoxicated man. He stopped drinking and started serving. He uprooted his family of six and moved from Pomeroy, Washington, to Seattle so that he could attend Bible College and prepare for the mission field. His wife Marjorie went to work as a nurse, and he took whatever job he could to supplement her income while he studied. Then they were commissioned as missionaries to Rhodesia (now Zimbabwe) where the Van Dykes became a living legend for their unflagging zeal for Christ and the Rhodesians.

Only their love for their youngest son could have forced them from the mission field to retirement in Arizona. Gregory was nearly killed in an automobile accident in Rhodesia, and his later needs prompted them to return to the United States.

Van had been working as a minister on our Central Christian staff for a little over a year when he learned of his deteriorating health.

He typically blamed no one but himself. "No one could have smoked as many cigarettes and consumed as much alcohol as I did without doing permanent damage to his body. I'm just grateful the Lord has let me live this long." He began making arrangements to reduce his work load; he needed more time at home, since he and Marjorie were going to be switching roles. She was returning to nursing; he would learn to keep house.

But he was not going to stop ministering. His work was becoming too exciting. "When I tell people that I have a new perspective on cancer now," he said, "they listen. And when I talk with very sick patients in the hospital, I can share Christ's mercy with them because I am experiencing what they are."

We talked frequently about his insight into Paul's acceptance of his own thorn in the flesh and his discovery that "When I am weak, then I am strong" (2 Corinthians 12:10). What impressed the rest of us was Van's abiding joy, his unshaken faith in God, and his almost eager anticipation of the next stage of his life. Heaven had always been his destination as a Christian, but now, as he neared it, he spoke with fervency. "I'm going home. Just think of all the friends I'll meet. I'll be waiting for you, too."

No one needed to explain to Van the meaning of Jesus' words. They were his hope and consolation:

"I am the resurrection and the life. He who believes in me will live, even though he dies; and whoever lives and believes in me will never die" (John 11:25, 26).

Jesus was speaking to His close friend Martha. Disconsolate over the loss of her brother Lazarus, and puzzled by—perhaps even critical of—Jesus' delay in coming until it was too late, Martha had no doubt that Jesus could have saved him. "If You had been here, my brother would not have died. [But You weren't, so he did.]"

In His answer to Martha Jesus summarizes the Christian's hope in death.

LIFE AND RESURRECTION
ARE FOUND IN JESUS

"I am the resurrection and the life." Jesus does not just give life; He *is* the life. Apart from Him life as God intended it cannot be found. Without Him the word *resurrection* has no meaning. Only those *in* Christ, *in* whom Christ dwells, experience living at its best. Those in Him will die and rise again with Him. Death no more has dominion over them, so they live without fear of dying.

I like the explanation given by a wise farmer whose preacher said he preached a better sermon on immortality than the preacher ever had. "Folks," he said, "you know how it is with a honeybee. He comes a buzzin' around and you dodge, scart you'll get stung. You git stung, anyways, but when you pick the bee's stinger out o' your hand, you ain't scart any more. You can reach up, play with that old buzzer! That honeybee's name is 'death.' But Jesus Christ's pulled out his stinger for us!"[1]

Paul has this in mind in Romans 6:3-11 when he reminds us that all who have been baptized into Christ's death will be raised with Him from the grave. There neither sin nor death has dominion over us. The stinger's been pulled!

Martha and Mary both have real faith in Christ—"If only you had been here . . ."—but they cannot comprehend that He can actually restore Lazarus to life.

Jesus' closest disciples share the sisters' faith in the Lord, but they, too, doubt His power over death. Later, when Jesus himself is placed in a tomb, they will forget all Jesus' teaching about His resurrection. They will accept His death as final, even though much earlier they had recognized He was teaching about *eternal life.* At a time when many of Jesus followers were deserting because of His strange teachings and growing unpopularity with the religious leaders, He asked the twelve, "You do not want to leave too, do you?" Peter answered for the group: "Lord, to whom shall we go? You have the words of eternal life" (John 6:67, 68). That's what he said. But Jesus' teaching about eternal life failed to prepare the twelve for Jesus' personal triumph over death. Jesus would prove that He could not be held by the tomb. Neither could Lazarus, once Christ took control. Neither will we.

I WILL NEVER DIE, EVEN THOUGH I DIE

"He who believes in me will live, even though he dies."

45

When I substitute *I* for "he who believes in me," I grasp the personal implication of Jesus' teaching. All of us like Shakespeare's Cleopatra have "immortal longings" in our souls, but with Jesus these longings become fact. The central doctrine of the Christian faith is that Jesus died and was buried—death is real and burial is real—and was raised from the grave by the power of God. Resurrection is real. Jesus proved that life is more than food and raiment; it embraces more than flesh and blood. It is not confined to this space or this time. As the giant telescopes have discovered galaxies our ancestors never imagined, and powerful microscopes have beheld miniscule worlds scientists have not yet fully explored, so Jesus' return from the grave opened up dimensions of reality and personality that no philosopher had ever taught.

And He made it available to you and me!

J. B. Phillips, whose modern language paraphrase of the Bible remains a favorite, recounts a dream that illustrates this.

As he lay in his hospital bed after surgery, he experienced an exhaustion so complete he was unable to move an eyelid. Yet he was conscious. He heard his doctor tell the night nurse, "I am afraid that he won't live till the morning." Phillips could say nothing. He could only lie helpless, with a feeling that he was resting on God, who seemed to be a kind of "sea of being" holding him up. Phillips was not afraid, for God seemed "infinitely compassionate and infinitely kind."

Then he fell asleep and dreamed vividly. He was trudging down a slope littered with human debris: ruined houses, cast-off shoes, rusty tin cans, discarded tires, rubbish. Ahead at a distance he saw a beautiful little valley. He ran toward it and came upon a narrow stream separating his cluttered slope from the gleaming valley. Across the stream was a white bridge, but he was prevented from crossing it by a smiling figure in white, who gently but authoritatively pointed Phillips back toward the miserable slope. He began to weep bitterly.

His nurse scolded."What are you crying for? You've come through tonight—now you're going to live!" Phillips could not explain his disappointment. She would not understand that he now appreciated the beauty that lay beyond death.[2]

His experience touches on Paul's description of the resurrection:

"So will it be with the resurrection of the dead. The body

that is sown is perishable, it is raised imperishable; it is sown in dishonor, it is raised in glory; it is sown in weakness, it is raised in power; it is sown a natural body, it is raised a spiritual body" (1 Corinthians 15:42-44).

The exact nature of this spiritual body is a matter of debate among Christians. What survives the grave? Whatever it is, it will be glorious, Paul affirms. I rather favor C. S. Lewis' guess that what will survive will be our senses. I should like to think that I'll be able to see, hear, touch, smell, and taste beyond the grave. We don't know, of course, but we can be assured that what lies ahead surpasses what lies around.

My conviction is somewhat like that of John Quincy Adams, whose famous reply to a friend inquiring of Adams' health on his eightieth birthday bears repeating:

"I thank you. John Quincy Adams is well. But the house in which he lives at present is becoming dilapidated. It is tottering upon its foundation. Time and the seasons have nearly destroyed it. Its roof is pretty well worn out. Its walls are much shattered and it trembles with every wind. I think John Quincy Adams will have to move out soon. But he himself is quite well, quite well."[3]

You could make a similar statement provided you believe that you will never die, even though you die.

I WILL LIVE WHILE I LIVE

When Jesus adds, "And whoever lives and believes in me will never die," He points to an enriched quality of life. Not everyone *lives and believes* in Him. It is fair to distinguish between living and existing. Real life does have *gusto,* though not the crude kind advertised by beer manufacturers. It has vitality, exudes joy, breathes hope, embraces love, and walks by faith. Christian faith enhances everything in life.

Unfortunately, millions continue to exist even after they have ceased to live. They don't believe in God, they don't believe in themselves, they don't look forward to tomorrow on earth or the day after tomorrow in eternity. They have no idea what Jesus means by abundant life.

Clarence Darrow speaks for some of them. A lifelong atheist, Darrow mused about his death. "Emotionally, I shall no doubt act as others do to the last moment of my existence. With my last breath I shall probably try to draw another. But

47

intellectually, I am satisfied that life is a serious burden, which no thinking humane person would wantonly inflict on someone else."[4]

Darrow is not alone. The late Bishop Bruce Baxter complained whimsically, "The trouble with life is it is so daily." Disraeli grumbled not so whimsically, "Youth is a blunder; manhood a struggle; old age a regret." What a contrast to life in Christ!

Christian faith does not always change life's circumstances, but it infuses them with meaning and makes victory possible. The Christian is an almost paradoxical character. He eagerly anticipates his life beyond the grave while at the same time enthusiastically plunging into meaningful activities here that he would prolong as long as possible. He entertains no death-wish. He wishes life. He will live as long as he lives.

He is like John Wesley, whose unshakable belief in Heaven enabled him to live all his life. When a lady asked him one day what he would do if he learned that he were going to die at midnight tomorrow night, he told her.

"Madam, I have an appointment to preach at Gloucester tonight and again at five in the morning. I would certainly keep those appointments. After that I would ride to Tewkesbury to preach in the afternoon and meet the societies in the evening. Then I would repair to my friend Martin's house for a meal and prayer. At ten o'clock I would commend myself to the Heavenly Father, lie down to rest, and wake up in glory."[5]

He would live while he lived.

Lester Van Dyke gave up everything he had, from the moment of his acceptance of Christ, to be a blessing to others in Christ's name. He and his equally committed wife had years ago adopted "Make Me a Blessing" as their theme song, he told me. He had given his strength to be a blessing; now in his sickness, he would give his weakness to be a blessing. He looked forward to Heaven, but as long as God would allow him to live, he would work and bless.

Either way, he is satisfied. He believes in Jesus; he accepts His teaching as God's eternal truth. He knows that what God did for Jesus in raising Him from the dead, and what He did through Jesus in raising Lazarus from the dead, He will do for every true believer. So as long as Van lives, he will live for Christ; and when he dies, he will live in Christ.

Several months after this was written, Van died. He died in the Lord, blessing us by his faith. He is satisfied

NOTES

[1]Grace Nies Fletcher, *Preacher's Kids.* New York: E. P. Dutton and Company, 1958, p. 224.

[2]J. B. Phillips, *For This Day,* ed. Denis Duncan. Waco: Word Books, 1974, pp. 32, 33.

[3]Quoted in Alistair MacLean, *High Country.* Charles Scribner's Sons, 1934.

[4]From Clarence Darrow, *The Story of My Life.* Quoted in E. Stanley Jones, *The Choice Before Us.* New York, Cincinnati, Chicago: The Abingdon Press, 1937, p. 67.

[5]John Wade, "Changing our Lives." *The Lookout,* March 15, 1981, p. 10.

HE PROMISES
A SURPRISING LIFE

John 12:20-28

Jesus is not the only great teacher who has taught that life can be found only by losing it. As Walter Lippmann has noted,

In all the great religions, and in all the great moral philosophies from Aristotle to Bernard Shaw, it is taught that one of the conditions of happiness is to renounce some of the satisfactions which men normally crave.[1]

His conclusion is echoed by another non-religious thinker, T. H. Huxley, the famous English biologist: "A man's worst difficulties begin when he is able to do as he likes."

The famed "Choice of Hercules" dramatizes these maxims. The hero of Greek mythology met two maidens at the turning of the road. The first voluptuously promised that if he would follow her, he would enjoy every pleasure of life. The other, of more modest dress and demeanor, offered a less attractive path. "I shall not deceive you," she told him. "The path I point out is full of labor, full of trials, full of difficulties; but it is a path that leads to immortality. If you seek to be beloved by your friends, you must serve your friends. If you desire to be honored by any city, you must benefit that city. If you wish to be admired by all Greece for your merit, you must endeavor to be of service to all Greece." Her name was Virtue. The only way to possess her was through renunciation.

This great moral lesson is acted out repeatedly in the pages of Scripture. Hebrews 11 offers a catalog of virtuous believers who renounced every other claim on them to serve God only. You know their names, because God has honored them: Abel, Enoch, Noah, Abraham, Moses, Rahab, and so on.

Other examples could be mentioned. Let me select just one from Acts 26. In Caesarea the apostle Paul was being held by Governor Festus. Paul had been first tried by the Sanhedrin, then by Governor Felix, then held in prison for two years because of his incredibly bold preaching. The new governor, Festus, then interviewed Paul and arranged a hearing for him before King Agrippa. Paul's defense turned into another courageous sermon, which was stopped by the shouting Festus,

"You are out of your mind, Paul! Your great learning is driving you insane."

Paul calmly answered Festus' outburst. "I am not insane." He explained the reasonableness of his remarks, turning for support to the King, who had some knowledge of Jewish beliefs and of the facts of Jesus' case. "King Agrippa, do you believe the prophets? I know you do."

A suddenly defensive King Agrippa replied, "Do you think that in such a short time you can persuade me to be a Christian?"

Paul's answer must have surprised him. He was a chained prisoner, penniless and without influence, in every way the contrast of the Emperor's appointed governor and king. "Short time or long—I pray God that not only you but all who are listening to me today may become what I am, except for these chains."

"I have learned to be content," Paul wrote elsewhere from prison (Philippians 4:11). In that same letter he exhorted his friends to "rejoice in the Lord always." He would rather have no chains, but he would not have them removed at the cost of compromise. He had found everything he wanted in life through his service to Jesus Christ.

Jesus speaks about the reasons for Paul's contentment in John 12:20-28. We must look closely at this surprising road to real living.

YOU GET BY GIVING

"I tell you the truth, unless a kernel of wheat falls to the ground and dies, it remains only a single seed. But if it dies, it produces many seeds." Without giving himself to His cross, Jesus cannot reproduce himself. As a seed can produce another plant with its many seeds only by giving itself to death, so Jesus can produce a crop of "saviors" for the world— servants of the Savior who will carry on His saving work on earth—only by giving himself up for their sake. "He must die to multiply himself."

Achievers in any field know that you can get what you want only by giving everything you have. Successful businessmen sacrifice everything for their business. What athlete has achieved lasting glory in his sport without sacrifice? What musician has enjoyed lasting fame without an endless, grueling effort to excel? And what Christian has achieved "saint-hood" without complete consecration?

By the way, I should speak a word of encouragement here to the Christian who despairs of accomplishing anything because he has few talents. "If only I could preach like Joe, or sing like Sally, or have the dynamic personality of Robert." You have it all wrong! You do not get by wishing, but by giving. Give away the little that you think you have. You'll be surprised how that little will grow. I like the way I heard it expressed: "The most miserable, pitifully smashed up life could blossom again *if it would only blossom for others."*

Try it. You get by giving.

Remember Jesus' brief encounter with the rich young man who was willing to do whatever was required to get eternal life—everything, that is, except the one thing necessary? "Teacher, what good thing must I do to get eternal life?" he asked Jesus (Matthew 19:16). His catalog of religious accomplishments was already quite impressive. He had fulfilled the commandments of the Law to the best of his ability and doubtless felt understandable pride in his correct life. Further, he had lots of money. He seemed to have the best of both worlds, the material and the spiritual.

Whether he was sincere is debatable. He may have felt unfulfilled and desired to do more for God, or he may have just been testing Jesus. Whatever his motive, he was not prepared to do the thing Jesus required. He could not give away his treasure in exchange for God's wealth. He went away sad—and he would live sad—because he would not accept the truth that you get by giving.

YOU LIVE BY DYING

"The man who loves his life will lose it, while the man who hates his life in this world will keep it for eternal life." Jesus is simply saying the same thing in a slightly different way. He has also expressed it somewhat differently on other occasions, speaking of cross-bearing (Mark 8:34f), serving God instead of money (Matthew 6:24), and hating others in order to be His disciple (Luke 14:26).

That word "hate" is a bother. Its powerful psychological and emotional overtones causes us to stumble. Surely Jesus isn't expecting us to turn against our loved ones, is He? No,

He isn't. He is, instead, stating in unmistakable terms that He demands our exclusive commitment. We are to disown or renounce any other claims to our allegiance, even our own claims, in order to follow Him. He wants to save our lives and, as J. B. Phillips translates His words, "The man who loves his own life will destroy it." You cannot expect to live by protecting yourself from risk, by comforting yourself in the warm embrace of your family, by dedicating yourself to the pursuit of money, or by anything else that this world's morality takes for granted. You have to die to what the world expects; only then will you really live.

Perhaps we can clarify this teaching by calling in the assistance of Socrates, who lived a few centuries before Christ. He saw the truth Jesus is expressing, even though he could not hope for the same reward Jesus offers. In his defense before the Athenian citizens who had condemned him for false teaching, Socrates addressed them,

> Someone will say: And are you not ashamed, Socrates, of a course of life which is likely to bring you to an untimely end? To him I may fairly answer: There you are mistaken: a man who is good for anything ought not to calculate the chance of living or dying; he ought only to consider whether in doing anything he is doing right or wrong— acting the part of a good man or of a bad.[2]

He must be dead to the opinions even of the judges who hold his life in their hands. He must be alive only to doing what is right.

A Hindu who had just heard the American missionary E. Stanley Jones speak caught the eternal implication of the Christian demand. In closing the meeting, he said, "If what the speaker has said tonight isn't true, it doesn't matter; but if it is true, then nothing else matters."[3]

He was speaking of the same missionary to whom a chaplain spoke as they sailed on board ship: "You don't drink? Why, you can't live in India without drinking."

Jones answered quietly, "Well, I don't have to live. I can always die. The Christian has that alternative. He can always die."[4]

This is a lesson the Christian will hear Jesus teach repeatedly: "You can die. Moreover, you must."

"What would happen to me," a man asked his friend, "if I

tried to carry on my business as Christ would want me to do it? I'd be ruined."

"And what will happen to you if you don't?" his friend told him. "What kind of ruin do you want?"

You live by dying.

YOU SUCCEED BY SERVING

"Whoever serves me must follow me; and where I am, my servant also will be. My Father will honor the one who serves me."

Everybody wants to know how to succeed in life. Advice is readily available: Set your goals, work hard, don't be detoured, associate with the right people, never forget Number One.

Once again Jesus' word is surprising. Forget Number One. "Follow me in service. Don't worry about success. If you serve me, my Father will honor you. That's success enough."

His is a hard word for aggressive, ambitious persons to hear. I am afraid Thackeray was describing more than Pendennis when he wrote that he, "having a most lively imagination, mistook himself for a person of importance very easily." We have similar imaginations and we want to succeed. We want to be served, not to serve; to lead, not to follow.

So we rebel. Like Milton's Satan, we would rather rule in Hell than serve in Heaven. C. S. Lewis has concluded that in the end there are only two kinds of people: those who say to God, "Thy will be done," and those to whom God says, "Thy will be done."[5] We may rule if we choose—but that is the road to Hell.

There is a kind of success, I suppose, in ruling in Hell, but not the kind Jesus promises. A moment's thought convinces us He's right. Who praises the pusher? Who really admires the self-server?

Winston Churchill touches this nerve in his history of World War II, borrowing his phrase from an earlier speech to entitle his second volume *Their Finest Hour.* It was also Britain's blackest hour, when she stood alone against Hitler's terrible onslaught. Churchill did not call his countrymen to glory nor to self-serving. He challenged them to serve, to fight in spite of overwhelming odds. Their finest hour was not in 1945 when victory was declared, but in their struggle against almost insuperable odds, when they served with no thought of self-glory.

Our century has honored no one more than Dr. Albert Schweitzer, who astonished his friends and the world when he turned his back on a career in theology and music to become a doctor in the heart of Africa. He was dead to the appeals of his friends to stay in Europe and pursue a glorious career; he was alive to Christ's call to serve. So he buried himself in his ministry—to be surprised by his growing fame.

Years later he visited America. When he arrived in New York on his first and only visit, even the hardened reporters were awed at the sight of the brawny but gentle doctor. One of them asked whether he regretted the sacrifice of his life to the natives of Africa. He answered, "There was no sacrifice. I am one of the greatly privileged."[6]

He wanted only to serve. He was amazed to discover himself among the honored.

If I were addressing a graduating class right now, I would select this Scripture. The students would probably not hear me gladly, any more than twenty centuries of mankind has heard Jesus. But those who will hear and apply His words—that you get by giving, you live by dying, you succeed by serving—will undoubtedly think they are sacrificing themselves to a high cause that leads them into danger, suffering, and even death. They may encounter all of these, of course, but they will also, perhaps to their surprise, discover that they are on the way to truth and life and that their least effort on Christ's behalf has been noted by the Father.

And the Father is eager to honor those who serve.

NOTES

[1]*A Preface to Morals.* New York: The Macmillan Company, 1929, p. 156.

[2]Plato, "Apology," *Five Great Dialogues,* B. Jowett, trans., Louise Ropes Loomis, ed. New York: Walter J. Black, 1942, p. 46.

[3]E. Stanley Jones, *A Song of Ascents.* Nashville: Abingdon Press, 1968, p. 112.

[4]Jones, p. 77.

[5]Roger Lancelyn Green and Walter Hooper, *C. S. Lewis, A Biography.* New York: Harcourt, Brace and Jovanovich, 1974, p. 222.

[6]Robert Payne, *The Three Worlds of Albert Schweitzer.* New York: Thomas Nelson and Sons, 1957, p. 214.

HE PROMISES
A POWERFUL LIFE

John 14:8-14

Can Jesus mean what He is saying? Is it possible that we can surpass His ministry?

Jesus makes remarkable claims for himself: "I am the way and the truth and the life"; "If you really knew me, you would know my Father as well"; "I am in the Father and the Father is in me." These assertions are mind-boggling in themselves, but then Jesus goes on to make claims *for us* that are amazing almost beyond belief. The simple statement and the promise contained in verse 12 require careful study, for Jesus is either misleading us or He is challenging us to demonstrate far more power than we have thought possible for us.

THE STATEMENT: "Anyone who has faith in me will do what I have been doing" (John 14:12a).

Jump to the end of John's Gospel to discover exactly what Jesus has in mind. Following His remarakble post-resurrection meal with the disciples, Jesus holds His famous conversation with Simon Peter, in which He asks Peter three times whether he really loves his Lord. When Peter repeatedly assures Him that he does, Jesus instructs him to "Feed my sheep."

Much is hidden in this deceptively simple exchange. Peter, who earlier disgraced himself when he denied even knowing Jesus at His trial, is quietly welcomed back into His Master's company. Once more Jesus reveals the forgiving, reconciling love of God. Peter is not to be a passive recipient of Jesus' love, however. If Peter really loves as Jesus loves, he can prove it through continuing Jesus' ministry. His Lord has been the Good Shepherd; now Peter must take up the shepherd's staff.

In the beginning Peter had answered when Jesus said, "Follow me." Jesus now repeats His invitation, but this time He does not mean for Peter to follow as a disciple follows his teacher, but to follow as a disciple one day *succeeds* his teacher. The time has come for Peter and his fellow disciples to fulfill their ministries.

His has been a ministry of preaching, teaching, healing, and miracle-working. His goal has been to save lives, to reconcile alienated men and women to God. His personal ministry is drawing to a close, but the need to rescue the lost remains. To succeed, Jesus must have successors. His disciples must now do what Jesus has been doing.

The apostle Paul so thoroughly grasped Jesus' meaning that he made it the rationale of his ministry:

"God was reconciling the world to himself in Christ, not counting men's sins against them. And he has committed to us the message of reconciliation. We are therefore Christ's ambassadors [His successors in the ministry of reuniting men and women with God, sent by Christ himself], as though God were making his appeal through us" (2 Corinthians 5:19, 20).

Paul is writing specifically of his apostolic mission. Jesus speaks more broadly, however: *Anyone* who has faith in Him will do what He has done. We can ask in prayer and know that He will grant it (14); we can draw upon the wisdom of the Holy Spirit to keep us true to Jesus' teachings and purposes (16, 26).

As Jesus is the Father's gift to mankind, so the Holy Spirit is Jesus' gift to His disciples to guide, strengthen, and teach them in Jesus' absence. The Holy Spirit also creates in the disciples a quality of life otherwise beyond our power, uniting us with one another in spite of our differences, making it possible for us to cooperate with each other to do the work that Jesus did. As He was a missionary from God to us, so we are missionaries from Christ to the world.

I read a few years ago of a judge in California who believed this and tried to conduct himself as judge in a way that was true to his Christ-appointed mission. He got himself into trouble!

Judge Hugh Wesley Goodwin, municipal court judge in Fresno, California, was investigated and finally thrown off the bench because he was allegedly mixing God and the law. His crime was in giving defendants a choice of going to church or to jail, in violation, his critics said, of the Constitution's clause on the separation of church and state. As a side issue, they were disturbed because he allowed a Thursday noon Bible study for courthouse employees to meet in his chambers. But the main charge was that in his year-and-a-half as judge, he granted persons guilty of minor crimes a choice of doing community service work, paying a fine, going to jail, or attending church services twice a week, one of which must feature a Bible study. Most chose the church option. Of approximately 200 persons who chose it, only five were returned on subsequent charges.

The judge did not fare well at the hands of his investigators. In this, too, he followed Jesus, who was constantly besieged by His critics and finally condemned to death in a rigged trial. I admire the judge, however, for trying to do through his profession what Jesus did in His: to rescue the lost, to bring them back to God, to restore them to full life. He knew that Christ had provided the way through His cross; what is now needed is to bring the guilty to that cross.

THE PROMISE: "He will do even greater things than these, because I am going to the Father" (John 14:12b).

Jesus is acknowledging the limits of human existence. Time and space have temporarily bound Him to first century Palestine. He can do only so much with so many. But the Holy Spirit, unchained by flesh and blood, can indwell whomever He chooses, driving those He empowers to accomplish what they could never do on their own, enabling them to love with superhuman love and to endure the unendurable for the sake of Christ.

Jesus in the flesh can curse the fig tree and make it wither (Mark 11:20-24), but the true believer can say to a mountain, "Go, throw yourself into the sea," and if he does not doubt, "it will be done for him." Not that *he* will accomplish this miraculous feat by his own power; no, he will draw on a higher power now accessible to one who has faith in Jesus.

In quantity Jesus' believers will accomplish more than He did just because there are more of us, in every land, continuing His ministry.

In quality God is now *in* us through the Holy Spirit, not just *with* us as when Jesus walked in flesh and blood. When the

Counselor (Holy Spirit) has come, Jesus promises, "on that day you will realize that I am in my Father, and you are in me, and I am in you."

"In Christ." This is undoubtedly the apostle Paul's favorite phrase. It sounds a little strange at first, until we remember that when someone says he is "in business," we know exactly what he means, and when he is "in love," we have no doubt about his condition. If he says he is "in debt," our defenses go up because we know what he'll ask next. My children's generation has changed the word to "into" (Are you "into" soul music, or "into" raquetball?), but the meaning is about the same. So when Paul writes, "If anyone is *in* (or *into*) Christ, he is a new creation" we understand. The new Christian is all wrapped up with, his thoughts saturated by, his goals identified with, his values similar to those of, Christ.

The New Testament leaves no doubt. If one is really a believer in Christ, then Christ lives in him, and so does the Holy Spirit. (See Galatians 2:20; Colossians 1:27; Romans 8:10, 11; 1 Corinthians 3:16.) Further, being in Christ is the same as being in the Spirit (Philippians 1:1; Romans 8:1, 9; Ephesians 2:22). If you believe in Christ and have learned to obey Him, your spirit is so intertwined with His that you have ceased to exist as an independent personality. You now live as an extension of Christ himself.

It is becoming clearer what Jesus is promising. When we live as extensions of Christ, the Spirit that empowered Him in the flesh will now empower His whole church, a body not limited to one place and one time, but able to inhabit the whole earth in every age. Yes, we can do even greater things!

Return to the end of John's Gospel one more time. At the beginning of the twenty-first chapter Jesus meets several of His disciples. They are returning empty-handed from a discouraging night of fishing. Instead of sympathizing with their plight, Jesus sends them right back to their fishing, giving them a strange order: "This time," He tells them, "throw your net on the right side of the boat." Obeying His instructions, they harvest such a catch they can't haul in the net.

Do you remember when Jesus first called these disciples to help Him? He invited just a few of them, promising to make them fishers of men. His "catch" was a small one. He could only satisfactorily disciple a limited group. Furthermore, apart from Him they could do nothing. When He specially commissioned them to go two by two on a healing and teaching expedition, they were successful. But when on their own they tried to heal a possessed boy, they failed (Mark 6:7-13; 9:14-19).

When they fished all night on their own, they also failed, but when they returned to the same waters empowered by Him, they were able to do marvelous things.

Jesus gave His attention to a small number of disciples. With them He was able to do some good. But when He withdrew His physical presence from them and empowered them with His Spirit, they could catch an abundance of men and women in the same manner as they had just caught the fish, with numbers far exceeding anything Jesus had done in the flesh.

The book of Acts proves Jesus right. On the Day of Pentecost alone, three thousand souls were added to the body. The disciples were able to do on that one day what Jesus had never done numerically. They were already doing greater works than He had done.

Bishop Gerald Kennedy of the Methodist church held a series of evangelistic meetings in his area some years ago. He reported that he was disturbed that Methodists were no longer any good at conversion. He heard fine choirs, listened to good hymn singing and offertory music, participated in the responsive readings, and observed that everything in the meetings was under control. That was just the problem, he said. "It is all under control—our control." The Spirit was absent—and so was the power. I rather agree with Sam Shoemaker of the Episcopal church, who wrote, "God is more eager that we should have spiritual power than we are to possess it."

What a difference that power can make, even to one man. You probably know the story of Dwight L. Moody's ministry. This humble layman was on his second visit to Europe in 1872 when, at an early morning meeting in a haymow near Dublin, he heard Henry Varley say quietly, "The world has yet to see what God can do with and for and through and in a man who is fully and wholly consecrated to him."

Moody could not get those words out of his mind. He was convinced that Varley meant any man. He didn't have to be educated or brilliant, qualifications which would have eliminated Moody. He just had to be a man, available. Moody was available. "By the Holy Spirit in me," he cried, "I will be one of those men."

He became the leading American instrument for the conversion of men and women to Christ in his generation, and his legacy still serves through the Moody Bible Institute, the Moody magazine, the Moody church, and other enterprises. He is living proof of Phillips Brooks' statement, "It does not take great men to do great things; it only takes consecrated men."

Christians now live in every land as successors to Jesus, carrying out His ministry through His Spirit, bringing the lost back to God, infiltrating the enemy stronghold to save the lost from certain death and lead them to certain life.

Today the body of Christ is doing greater things than the disciples who first listened to Jesus could imagine.

He has kept His promise of a powerful life.

HE PROMISES
ANSWERED PRAYER

John 14:13, 14

This chapter is really Part 2 of Chapter 8. The power that Jesus promises in John 14:12 He makes available through the prayers He invites us to pray in verses 13 and 14. Verse 14 sounds so appealing that we are tempted to memorize it and apply it at will: "You may ask me for anything. . . ."

THE PURPOSE OF PRAYER

You have no doubt heard of the old mountaineer who was standing outside his shack, watching the smoke billow out.

"Hey!" a passing motorist yelled as he slammed on his brakes. "Your house is on fire!"

"Yep," the old man answered.

"Well, aren't you going to do anything about it?" the motorist yelled back.

"I'm doin' somethin' about it. I'm praying for rain."

If he had wanted to, he could have buttressed his case by pointing out several Biblical instances in which prayer effected amazing results. Remember Paul and Silas in prison at Philippi, to mention one example? They had healed a possessed slave girl whose owners made their fortune by exploiting her affliction. To get even, the owners stirred up a crowd and dragged Paul and Silas to the magistrates, charging them with "advocating customs unlawful for us Romans to accept or practice" (Acts 16:21). The two men were stripped, beaten, and thrown into jail, where they were confined to an inner cell and fastened in stocks.

Instead of bemoaning their fate, however, Paul and Silas prayed and sang hymns to God until around midnight, when a violent earthquake shook the foundations of the prison, opened the doors, and loosened everybdy's chains. Maybe the old mountaineer wasn't as foolish as he seemed. If God could send an earthquake for Paul and Silas, couldn't He send the oldtimer some rain? Didn't Jesus say "anything"?

When our family lived in Indianapolis, I enjoyed reading Tom Keating's columns in the *Star.* One of his best was an account of answered prayer. The pastor of Saints Peter and Paul Cathedral had received the bad news that an underground pipe connecting the church with the main beneath the street had broken, causing severe loss of pressure in the area. It had to be fixed immediately. Not surprisingly, the water company decided the church should pay the $3980 repair bill.

At one time that would not have been such a burden, but the cathedral, which in its heyday in the 1940s and 1950s counted more than 5,000 parishioners, had hit hard times and now numbered fewer than 600 members, mostly poor. Father Minta did not know what to do, except pray. So he prayed.

At ten o'clock the next morning, an elderly couple stopped by to drop off a donation in memory of a deceased relative. They gave Minta $3,000 in one-hundred-dollar bills.

An hour later the mail arrived. The first letter he opened was from a couple who lived outside the parish. It contained a $1,000 donation. The church had just made a $20 profit.[1]

Should we be surprised? Didn't Jesus say anything?

I'm certain you could recount some prayer stories like these. You probably have some others, too; these are stories of unanswered prayers, ones which called for more urgent responses from God but which He seemed to ignore. Does Jesus really mean *anything*?

Look again. He promises, "Whatever you ask in my name, so *that the Son may bring glory to the Father."* He may not send rain on the mountain shack, but if His purposes can best be served by releasing Paul and Silas from prison, an earthquake is not too much to ask for. God receives glory or honor when His purposes are fulfilled, when His kingdom's work is being accomplished. There are times, though, when even His best people do not get what they ask for.

When Jesus asked for possible release from His appointment with the cross, His request was refused. The kingdom required the cross. When Paul pleaded with God three times to be released from his infirmity (2 Corinthians 12:7-10), God did not grant his request. Paul accepted God's decision, concluding that his thorn kept him "from becoming conceited because of these surpassingly great revelations."

God has obligated himself to keep His word, and He will do so, but He has never promised to grant our every wish if we are seeking only our personal benefit. A Christian has really ceased to live just for himself, anyway. He has entered a larger world, the kingdom of God, in which his desires are intermingled with God's. To seek only personal good is to ask God to play favorites.

If this is true, then we must return to our question: What does Jesus mean by "anything"?

Read both the thirteenth and the fourteenth verses again. Jesus does not promise to dispense favors willy-nilly, but to act in harmony with His life's purpose. He wants to bring glory to His Father. He is still on the same subject that we studied in the last chapter, still assuring His disciples that "anyone who has faith in me will do what I have been doing," and "even greater things" will he do. Further, he will accomplish them through Jesus' power, not his own. Jesus wants His ministry to continue. He is waiting to be asked for His help. The "anything," then, must bring honor to the Father.

Martin Luther literally claimed this promise. In 1540 his good friend Frederick Myconius lay dying. Sensing that his end was near, with a weak and trembling hand he wrote a letter to Luther. When the latter read it, he immediately dispatched this reply:

"I command thee in the name of God to live, because I still have need of thee in the work of reforming the church. . . . The Lord will not let me hear while I live that thou art dead, but will permit thee to survive me. For this I am praying. This is my will, and may my will be done, because *I seek only to glorify the name of God.*"

When Myconius sent his letter, he had already lost his power of speech. Within a short time after hearing from Luther, he regained it and his complete health. He outlived Luther by two months.[2]

Luther sought "only to glorify the name of God." Jesus sought the same: "That the Son may bring glory to the Father."

As I was meditating on this verse, the telephone rang. My wife was calling about money. I was not receptive. Lately the bills have been horrendous. Our three teenagers need money for food for their youth choir tour, she said, and our son's camp registration with its $40 fee is overdue. We agreed on a way to provide food money for the tour, but I balked at the

64

registration fee. I have to draw the line somewhere, I told her, and I don't have the money.

That was the end of the conversation, but not of my thoughts on the subject. Before long I relented. He must go to camp even if I have to borrow the money. How can I hope that *my* son will grow up to "bring glory to the Father" if I am unwilling to make the personal sacrifices necessary to insure that he receives the best possible instruction in the Father's will? Christian summer camp is not an option, but an integral part of his Christian education.

I had no sooner made my decision than I thought of Jesus' words in the Sermon on the Mount (Matthew 7:9-11):

> "Which of you, if his son asks for bread, will give him a stone? Or if he asks for a fish, will give him a snake? If you, then, though you are evil, know how to give good gifts to your children, how much more will your Father in heaven give good gifts to those who ask him!"

For his good, I could not deny my son. I want him to become the best possible person, so I will see that what he needs he receives. For *my* good, God will not deny me. The key, of course, is "good." Jess Moody says that God answers prayer in four ways: Yes, No, Later, and You've got to be kidding! Had the request been for a video game or a motorcycle or one of the hundreds of other "essentials" which my son periodically asks for, the answer would have been one of the last three, probably the last. But the request was for his good.

Lane doesn't get everything he asks from me. He has to go to school, even when he asks not to. He has to be faithful in church activities, has to brush his teeth, has to do his chores around the house, has to do without some things. Sometimes he must think he doesn't get anything he wants from me. Some of his "prayers" are not granted.

Neither are some of mine. Like Paul, I have wrestled with some minor health problems all my life. God does not take them away. Even worse, I have constantly embarrassed myself with some temperament problems—too quick to cry, too quick to get angry. Then there have been periods of financial stress, and bleak days in the church when I have felt all alone and misunderstood, or even worse, incompetent. I have prayed but have not seen immediate answers.

Yet through them all, I am forced to admit, He has consistently answered according to my best interests. I am better for His answers than for my requests.

THE POSSIBILITIES IN PRAYER

Thus I am beginning to understand the possibilities in prayer. "Whatever you ask in my name" means asking in accordance with all His name stands for, asking as one united with Him through faith, asking as one who wants to accomplish Christ's desires and purposes. He cannot promise to give what would be contrary to His character or what would have undesirable effects, either in the petitioner or in the kingdom.

The Bible often uses "in the name of" to mean "by the power of." When the crowds shouted to Jesus as He entered Jerusalem, "Blessed is he who comes in the name of the Lord!" (Matthew 21:9), they were acknowledging the *power* of God in Jesus. To act in God's name is to act with God's authority. To act in the name of the law is to have the authority to perform deeds authorized by that law.

The long-honored tradition, now being more frequently challenged, of a bride's taking the name of her husband symbolizes the same thing. She has carried her father's name because he is the one who has had authority over her. In assuming her husband's name, she signals that he is now the head of her house. In the current liberation movement many women refuse to accept their husband's names; they will not acknowledge that their husbands have any authority over them.

When we put on Christ's name, we submit to His authority. To assume His name without yielding to His will is hypocrisy. To wear His name is to live His life, share His dreams, help His cause, follow His leading. When we ask in Christ's name, then, we desire to be *in* Him and ruled *by* Him. There is consistency between life and request, between work and want.

A minister learned this on the golf course. His partner was a priest, who blessed himself before successfully one-putting each hole. The minister regularly two- or three-putted. After a few holes, he announced, "I think I will cross myself before I putt." So he did at the next hole, but even after he crossed himself, he still three-putted it. So he said to the priest, "Why doesn't crossing myself work for me the way it works for you?"

The priest's answer is good theology: "It doesn't mean a thing if you can't putt." There has to be consistency between life and prayer. Jesus never promised to perform miracles for an undisciplined golfer.

So we must be careful with Jesus' promise of answered prayer. A woman stopped attending church. She had prayed for her seriously ill mother to recover, but her mother died anyway. The woman could not handle what she called "this rejection." A man prayed for money to take him through a financial crisis. He could not raise the money, so he lost his business—and his faith.

Before deserting Jesus for promising what He does not deliver, they should return to the Scriptures to study His prayers. He does not pray for anything for himself except to be kept in union with His Father and for help to do His Father's will. He offers to do extravagant things for His disciples, yet He himself lives simply, devoting himself completely to the kingdom. In the end He is rewarded with the finest answer of all, His resurrection from the grave and ascension into eternal life with the Father. His prayer reminds us that, as John Killinger has said, "Prayer is not an ordering service with a divine bellhop at the other end. It is communion."[3]

But if it is communion, then the pray-er must beware of the risks. He runs the risk, as Paul Scherer has written, of "growing more like Jesus of Nazareth." At first that sounds appealing, until we realize all it implies. It means

> to love where love is sacrificed, to be unselfish where the crowd will take advantage of your unselfishness, cheat you for being honest, and hurt your feelings for showing yourself affectionate![4]

A risk. But the alternative is less appealing: to become unlike Christ!

God is not our divine bellhop. Jesus is not an indulgent friend ready to cater to our every whim. The Lord has His purposes. Those who believe in Him will be continuing the work of Jesus. He will do anything we ask to fulfill that ministry and to bring glory to the Father.

We pray, therefore, with the hope that our desires are God's desires.

Once, when President Lincoln was meeting a delegation at the White House, a minister in the line told him he "hoped the Lord is on our side."

The President quickly responded, "I don't agree with you." Then to the suddenly quiet group he continued, "I am not at all concerned about that, for we know that the Lord is always on the side of the right. But it is my constant anxiety and prayer that I and this nation should be on the Lord's side."[5]

"Whatever you ask in my name," if it is on the Lord's side, the right side, if it will help you do what Jesus has been doing—if, in other words, it brings glory to the Father—He will do it for you.

NOTES

[1]Thomas R. Keating, "Power of Prayer Proved." *Indianapolis Star,* November 21, 1977.

[2]Peter Marshall, *John Doe, Disciple.* New York: McGraw-Hill Book Company, 1963, p. 184.

[3]John Killinger, *For God's Sake Be Human.* Waco: Word Books, 1970, p. 131.

[4]Paul Scherer, *Love Is a Spendthrift.* New York: Harper & Brothers, 1961, p. 55.

[5]Carl Sandburg, *Abraham Lincoln: The War Years,* Vol. 3. New York: Harcourt, Brace & Company, 1939, p. 346.

HE PROMISES
AN ADVENTUROUS LIFE

Matthew 28:16-20

I can't remember when I did not know the Great Commission. We memorized it in Sunday school when I was a child; we frequently heard stirring—and not so stirring—sermons on this text at camp, in conferences, and in worship services. I thought I had learned everything there was to know about Matthew 28:16-20.

This study on the promises of Jesus has changed my mind. I have not been aware of the promises implied in the Commission. One promise is explicit: companionship with Christ. "Surely I will be with you always . . ." is a pledge which Christian workers have always counted on.

Other implied promises easily escape our attention. We usually concentrate on Jesus' authority, on His orders to His disciples, and on the needs of the world, but we seldom consider what happens to the person who obeys Jesus' Commission. In an era of aimless living Jesus promises a goal-oriented life. The true disciple will waste no time wringing his hands over what to do with his life. He knows. He is to make disciples. In an age which urges a quest for meaning, Jesus' disciple does not question whether his life has meaning. His life gains a sense of purpose and value to the extent that he obeys Jesus' orders. Most exciting of all, Jesus promises ever-expanding horizons to His followers. To make disciples of all nations is to leave home spiritually, if not geographically, to think in kingdom terms, to embrace the whole inhabited earth as one's field of service.

When one is under the Commission, he is liberated from boredom; he finds himself ever growing, always seeking to serve.

On a recent vacation trip I enjoyed happy reunions with many Christian friends whose lives are proof of these promises: a preacher friend in the Mid-South region has never lived anywhere else, but his vision is as broad as the world itself; a country doctor in Kentucky who has served the same small region for more than forty years, whose love for his people is transparent, and whose joy in serving others for Christ's sake is contagious; a fellow minister in a large city, who is courageously battling the evil of urban blight to bring the gospel to people of all races and economic conditions; an executive secretary of a mission agency who has found complete satisfaction in assisting missionaries all over the earth. All these enjoy a zest for living that is infectious.

ADVENTUROUS LIVING BEGINS WITH CHRIST'S ORDERS

It is possible to be a faithful, pew-sitting church member all your life and never experience Christ's promised excitement in life. You cannot grasp your Christianity like a spiritual security blanket and know anything at all about adventurous living. You can blithely read over the Great Commission, conclude that Jesus had somebody else in mind, return to business as usual, and never be fully satisfied with your life. You cannot respond to Jesus' orders the way Moses initially answered God's call to free the Israelites and expect to receive everything He has in store for you.

Think of Moses for a minute. Better yet, reread Exodus 3 and 4, a dramatic narrative of Moses' encounter with God in the burning bush, and compare Moses' reaction to God with ours to Christ.

God plans to rescue His people, the slave-nation Israel, from the clutches of Egypt's Pharaoh. He orders Moses to lead Israel to freedom.

Moses is appalled. His sense of inferiority recoils at the idea that he should become a leader in saving God's people. "Who am I, that I should go to Pharaoh?" Our automatic reaction to God's orders seems always to be, "I can't do it. I am not able!"

Moses worries about his poor speaking ability. God wants him to speak to Pharaoh, obviously the job of a talented orator, not a tongue-tied shepherd. "O Lord, I have never been eloquent. . . . I am slow of speech and tongue." Christ's command also seems to require communication skills—yet He does not limit His commission to the eloquent.

Moses doubts he will be believed. "What if they do not believe me or listen to me and say, 'The Lord did not appear to you'?" Who has ever started out to fulfill Christ's commission without wondering what to say to the scoffers and doubters?

He is even unsure of his knowledge of God. When they ask

him God's name, he wonders, "What shall I tell them?" Who has ever felt adequate to speak to others about Christ when his own knowledge of Him seems so shaky?

So we answer Christ's commission in the same language with which Moses answers God, "O Lord, please send someone else to do it." God prevails in Moses' life, however, and all subsequent history knows of the adventurous life of this man of God. Once Moses accepts the authority of God, life is never again the same for him.

Our argument with Christ resembles that of Moses with God, but all our objections do not change the fact: if we want to be Christ's disciples, we must obey His orders. The "very end of the age" has not yet arrived. Everybody has not yet been reconciled to God. Our assignment is to bring them back to the God who made and loves them. It is for their sake that we obey Christ.

In obeying, we reap the promise of an adventurous life. We make disciples of others—and discover *ourselves* growing in ways we had not anticipated. We baptize others into the death, burial, and resurrection of Christ—and find *ourselves* dying to our old selfishness and being raised into finer persons. We teach others—and *we* learn more than those we teach.

We do everything for the sake of Christ and others—and awake to the excitement of a life of adventure.

Through it all we enjoy His constant companionship. We feel protected by His presence, as Martin Luther did. Standing before the Holy Roman Emperor, Charles V, who warned Luther that the princes of Germany would abandon his Reformation cause and tried to frighten him by asking, "Where will you be then?" Luther answered straight from the Commission: "Right where I am now, in the hands of Almighty God."

EARLY CHRISTIANS LED ADVENTUROUS LIVES

The Acts of the Apostles could more appropriately have been titled, *Adventures of the Apostles.* These spirit-filled disciples were obviously having the time of their lives as they devoted themselves to carrying out Christ's commission. Reread Acts with the promise of an adventurous life in mind. From the first chapter, with its description of the disciples awaiting the coming of the Holy Spirit, through the last chapter, in which Paul awaits his trial before Caesar, you will read of vibrant, excited Christians caring for nothing so much as obeying God rather than men and experiencing anything but boredom. Their adventure is launched on the Day of Pentecost (chapter 2) with the thrilling miracle of communication which resulted in the baptism of three thousand persons. It leads to imprisonment for the leaders (John and Peter, chapter 3), the opportunity of preaching before the assembled religious and civil leaders (chapter 4), the privilege of walking by faith in God as individual Christians sell what they possess in order to insure that no Christian will be without life's physical necessities (chapters 2 and 4), the martyrdom of Stephen, who counted it an honor to die for Christ (chapter 7), and the transformation of the Christian-hater (Paul) into the greatest Christian-maker. You will read of miraculous escapes from prison, persecutions, debates, tender moments of affection, shipwrecks, trials, healings, and other adventures. You will discover nothing boring about these disciples' lives.

The adventures are not limited to the "big names" in early Christianity, either. You will read about Aquila, a humble tentmaker, and his wife Priscilla, whose faith in Christ takes them from Pontus, Italy, to Corinth and on to Ephesus to serve the Commission. These eager students of God's Word soon become teachers; the humble tentmakers soon play key roles as important church-builders. The adventures of the Commission come to every Christian, whether he moves or stays at home, to the extent that he serves his Lord.

ADVENTUROUS CHRISTIANS STILL OBEY HIS ORDERS— AND ENJOY HIS PROMISES

On March 7, 1981, Chester Bitterman III, a Bible transalator in Colombia, who was part of a team working to reduce thirty-three Indian languages to writing, was killed by left-wing terrorists, who accused him of being a spy for the CIA. His 109 fellow translators were offered immediate return to the United States when it became apparent that they were also in danger. Not one of the workers left the field. They would not be intimidated by the terrorists' threats.

"I am willing to go anytime the Lord calls me," one of the translators said. "We all came here with the idea that we might go home in a box, but now this possibility seems more real. There's never been a time like this for growing in the Lord." They are living daily with the possibility of following Bitterman to their deaths, but they speak of growth and not of fear.

Another colleague added, "We are all carrying on with our task per usual, even overtime, as we may not have much time to reach the tribespeople." He expresses fear—not for his life but for the people who might not be saved if he fails to complete his translation before being killed.

What of Bitterman's parents, who could be bitter that their son, employed in such noble work, is dead? His mother expressed no remorse: "There's a lot more involved than the life of our son; there are the lives of thousands of Indians in the jungle who have never heard the story of Jesus."[1] Other Bittermans prepared to replace Chester on the Colombia team.

Bitterman's death reminds us that adventure always involves risk. Jesus does not promise that it will be easy to carry out His orders, but He does promise to be with us. On the strength of that assurance, Bitterman and countless other Christians have courageously accepted Jesus' commission and, to borrow Oswald Chambers' phrase, have "smilingly washed their hands of the consequences." Their task is to obey; God's responsibility is to take care of the consequences.

For this reason Christians often seem to have thrown caution to the wind. Super-cautious personalities never know the joys of adventurous living. They need, as Ralph Waldo Emerson stated, to "give their heart a holiday from caution." They need to go where they have never been before, to try what they have never done before, to speak as they have never spoken before. Only then will they feel totally alive. They can do all this and more, if they will trust the consequences to God.

Dag Hammerskjold, the late great secretary-general of the United Nations, jotted in his *Markings,*

"—Lead us not into temptation,
But deliver us from evil:
Let all that is in me serve Thee,
And *thus* free me from all fear."[2]

Ours is but to serve; His is to banish fear.

I think it is in Ralph Connor's *Black Rock* that Leslie Graeme admires Craig, who fearlessly ministers to the rough men in his lumber camp. "What a trump he is!" Graeme exclaims. "And without his religion, he'd be pretty much like the rest of us!"

That is the point exactly. Our religion—our trust in the Lord—is what separates us from the mass of fearful humanity. We don't have to be afraid—we are on a permanent holiday from timidity.

I am thinking now of many friends whose lives are adventurous because they care for nothing except serving. They serve on mission fields around the world—and right here at home. They are married and single, ordained ministers and "just laymen" (as some of them speak of themselves). They would not allow me to call attention to them on these pages because they see nothing remarkable in their lives. They would confess, however, to having a wonderful time serving the Lord.

I must tell you about one, though. Years ago Beth Alice Johnson and her husband Don answered God's call to serve Him in Ethiopia. This vivacious, city-loving woman found herself in the bush country, serving under conditions she could never have imagined earlier. Unfortunately, she had to return home because of the worsening kidney disease which would eventually claim her life. Before her death she wrote her friends in the Christian Missionary Fellowship. She was recovering from cataract surgery in both eyes and was confined to her wheelchair because of her weakness. Medicines had destroyed her voice—and she had always loved to sing. In her letter she included, among others, these two paragraphs which I wish to quote here.

> "I'm often asked if I'd do it again, knowing I'd end up a semi-invalid with kidney disease. I don't have to give it one second's thought to say most emphatically—"Yes." I'd go with the same husband and kids, live in the same tent under my same old thorn tree and do it all over again. The blessings of this illness have so outweighed the adversities that it is impossible for me to praise God fully for all that He has done for me."

That paragraph was about her. This one is for us.

> "None of us knows how many days are left to us on this

earth. For some of us it may be a few weeks, for some—many years. So it seems so important that each day finds us growing in the Lord, drawing closer to Him, giving up more of ourselves to Him and investing our energies, time, and money in reaching all around the world to those who don't yet know our Savior with His precious message of love and forgiveness for all."

Shortly after writing these words, she died. What is remarkable in this dying woman's testimony is what she does not write. She utters no words of bitterness or regret. She blames no one for her kidney disease, she does not grieve over the loss of the comforts she was accustomed to in America, and she has no longing for what might have been. Instead, as one who long before placed herself under Christ's authority, she has done what she believed the Lord wanted her to do and has found more blessings than she could find adequate words with which to praise God.

Hers has been an adventurous life.

NOTES

[1]"Good News for Columbia—at All Costs." *Eternity, May 1981, p. 10.*
[2]Dag Hammerskjold, *Markings.* New York: Alfred A. Knopf, 1964, p. 125.

HE PROMISES A PEACEFUL LIFE

John 14:27; Romans 5:1-11

Ours has not been called the "Age of Anxiety" without reason. G. K. Chesterton describes the modern mind as being "like a motor-car on a lonely road which two amateur motorists have been just clever enough to take to pieces but are not quite clever enough to put together again."[1] They know something is very wrong with themselves, but they do not know how to repair it.

They devour countless books and articles that teach anxious persons how to banish anxiety. If they will only apply this prescription or follow that suggestion, they will become the perfect person they dream of becoming. But perfection eludes them and depression, loss of self-control, troubled relationships, and a dangerously low self-esteem defeat them. There is no peace.

So they turn to the psychiatrist for help. He advises them to stop struggling and to think more highly of themselves than they do. In the psychiatrist's office they become tranquil, but when they return to their troubled environments, anxiety returns with a vengeance. They need something more than the psychiatrist can give.

Jesus is speaking to them: "Peace I leave with you; my peace I give to you. I do not give to you as the world gives [(they have tried that peace and found it to be no peace)]. Do not let your hearts be troubled and do not be afraid."

In many ways, Dagwood is the perfect representative of the average man's frustrations. I follow his troubles faithfully, seeing my own existence mirrored in his. One Sunday's strip stopped me dead, however, because it was so out of character. When he prepares to take his bath, Blondie tells him she won't let anybody disturb him. As he leaves the house, he reassures the postman—whom he so often overruns as he dashes for work—that he is safe this morning because Dagwood has plenty of time. He doesn't have to run to catch his bus; he arrives at work five minutes early, to the amazement of other employees. Mr. Dithers greets Dagwood with the news that he is giving him a big raise and a promotion because he did such a brilliant job on the McGraw contract. In addition, Dithers gives him a $100 bonus and the day off. When he returns to his house, he meets a man at the door who is not a salesman but someone giving away free samples. Then Herb, best friend and next door neighbor, comes over to ask him if he can play poker at Berl's garage. Blondie overhears the conversation and, instead of throwing her usual objections, tells Dagwood to stay out as late as he wants to and to have a good time. At the poker game, Dagwood draws a royal flush and cleans up from the other players.

This is not the Dagwood I know. Gone is the harried, frustrated, henpecked, ineffective man whose everyday experiences reflect the annoyances which keep him and the rest of us from experiencing peace. In the last panel, Blondie clears up the reader's confusion: "After fifty years of this comic strip, he deserves a day like today."[2]

The humor is in the unbelievable peace Dagwood experiences in the one day in which everything goes his way. There is no doubt about it, Dagwood deserves such a day. But is his perfect day what Jesus means by peace?

PEACE IN TIME OF TROUBLE

On August 7, 1945, an American bomber took off from a little island in the Pacific Ocean and headed for Japan. A few hours later a parachute descended over the city of Hiroshima, dropping a weapon of war unlike anything ever known to man. In a moment a blinding flash followed by a terrific explosion killed 78,000 persons and injured more than 37,000. America had dropped its first atomic bomb on a major population center.

"The United States of America now possesses a weapon with unparalleled power, a weapon that will make us invulnerable to attack so long as we alone possess it," scientists told us. It was a feat designed to insure peace in the world and peace in the American heart. From that moment, however, Americans have been seized with a fear greater than they had ever known before. A country that could kill on such a gargantuan scale can be killed in turn. It is only a question of time. No matter how many bombs are in our stockpiles, no matter how many billions we spend for defense, we cannot buy peace.

What is true in the world is true in our neighborhoods.

Americans are buying guns at an accelerating rate, hoping to protect themselves from the increasing violence of this crazy society. The rise in gun sales is accompanied by a predictable rise in homicides and suicides. The world seeks peace through self-protection. That is not the peace Jesus promises.

In this century nations have risen and fallen with amazing suddenness. In 1911 Bertrand Russell wrote a book mentioning the Emperor of China. There had always been an emperor in China, clear back beyond the dawn of written history. But while his book was in print, the emperor fell. Russell changed the book in his second edition, replacing the Emperor of China with the Emperor of Germany. That emperor fell. Then Russell made another change, speaking this time of the Emperor of Japan. He has not fallen, but his power has been stripped from him, and he is simply a figurehead in that newly democratic country. You cannot count on empires nor upon governments of any kind to establish peace.

When I was a public school student, I studied geography. Much of what I learned then is obsolete now. I memorized the names of countries that no longer exist; I learned to admire the British Empire, for example, an empire that has evaporated. Missionaries have left America for countries in Africa like the Congo and Rhodesia, but they returned from Zaire and Zimbabwe. And in the Middle East perpetual wars destroy any hope for global peace. Not as the world gives does Jesus give peace.

What Jesus means may be observed in action in Acts 27. The apostle Paul was aboard ship on his way to Rome to be tried by the Emperor. They were sailing late in the season, when dangerous storms drove sea-wise captains and their crews to dock their ships and wait for fairer weather. Paul foresaw a disastrous voyage ahead and warned against traveling. But because "the harbor was unsuitable to winter in, the majority decided that we should sail on, hoping to reach Phoenix and winter there."

They didn't make it. Soon they were caught up on a "northeaster," a wind of hurricane force that battered the boat mercilessly, forcing the crew to cast the cargo overboard and then to give up any hope of being saved. Only Paul stood among them with peace that passes understanding. God had spoken to him and assured him that he would reach Caesar and that everyone traveling with him would be safe, although the ship would run aground.

You can read the rest of the story. Paul's predictions were fulfilled to the letter. What is remarkable is the peace with which he communicated his intelligence to the men. From his close walk with God he had received a reservoir of strength that enabled him to withstand, without panic, the worst the storm could throw at him, like his own Master, who had the ability to sleep in a storm that terrorized His disciples (Mark 4:35-41). This is not a peace that the world gives.

PEACE WITH GOD

The source of peace of mind is God. Without His abiding presence in the midst of storms, all the encouraging words of friends and leaders are powerless. The famous actress of an earlier era, Mary Pickford, published a book she entitled, *Why Not Try God?* At first blush the title seemed harmless enough. Then I read Professor Halford Luccock's stinging rebuttal to her shallow thinking about God. "Why not try aspirin?" he asked. He was objecting to treating God like a wonder drug for easing this or that pain. When we point to God as the source of personal peace, we mean much more than "trying God." God delivers His promises only on His terms, not on ours. He promises peace, but these are the conditions:

"Therefore, since we have been justified through faith, we have peace with God through our Lord Jesus Christ, through whom we have gained access by faith into this grace in which we now stand" (Romans 5:1, 2).

The peace comes through Christ . . . *by faith.* It is a result of God's act *of grace,* not something we can earn or guarantee for ourselves.

Note our condition before Christ saved us:

we were still powerless (6),
we were ungodly (6),
we were still sinners (8),
we were objects of God's wrath (9),
we were God's enemies (10).

Contrast our prior condition with our present one, made possible through Christ's saving act:

we have been justified (1, 9),
we have peace with God (1),

we have access to God (2),
we live by God's grace (2),
we can rejoice even in suffering (3),
we live in God's love (5),
the Holy Spirit lives in us (5),
we shall be saved (9, 10),
we are reconciled to God (10, 11).

Here is the source of our sense of well-being in Christ. We have been accepted by God! We do not have to worry—He will take care of us! When we worry, we act as if we expect God to leave us in the lurch. If we try to do everything in our own strength, we rebuff His desire to help us.

Yet many of us are like a typical young man, proud of his stamina and ability, who gets what he wants by the strength of his will. He works his way through college and launches his career. Everything goes his way. He is talented, ambitious, energetic, successful—and proud.

Then he crashes. His business affairs are not going as well as he dreamed; his family is wracked by tension, and his wife blames him. He can't sleep; he feels depressed, has difficulty forcing himself to the office, begins drinking heavily, and is always anxious, distracted, and upset. He tries to solve his problem the way he has always tackled every difficulty: he works harder and longer hours. But instead of making things better, his situation worsens.

It is not that he is short of money. He has all he needs. He could take a vacation, but his last holidays were no help; they just afforded him more time to worry. What can he do? Where can he find peace?

The fact is, there is little he can do until he finds the source of his peace in God. He does not need to try harder; he needs to relax into God's power. He needs to hear the truth the psalmist sang:

"Blessed is the man
who does not walk in the counsel of the wicked
or stand in the way of sinners
or sit in the seat of mockers.
But his delight is in the law of the Lord,
and on his law he meditates day and night.
He is like a tree planted by streams of water . . ."
(Psalm 1:1-3).

The tree takes its nourishment from the water-soaked soil. It does not toil or fret, but lets the waters flow through it. Its strength is derived from remaining in the source of its life.

My wife has taught me this little lesson through her new bank account. For years we lived precariously close to financial disaster, and at times we have written checks accidentally on "non-sufficient funds." God has always provided everything we have needed—but not always everything we have wanted, especially at the end of the month! The usual tranquility of our domestic scene has more than once been disturbed when a righteously indignant husband has demanded to know why he should pay for checks written on money that was not in our bank account—thus absolving himself of all blame!

Joy has solved the problem. She now banks with a modern bank that has a unique feature: it allows her to write up to several hundred dollars worth of checks which the bank will cover until she makes her deposit. They advertise it as worry-free banking; this special account provides automatic reserves for time of crisis.

That is what a firm relationship with God through Christ does—it gives us reserves for the crisis. He is our strength and ever present help in time of need. We may be unconscious of our need for Him, even as we are torn asunder by conflicts and complexes that only He can cure. To draw near to God through Christ is to turn over to Him our hidden resentments, bitterness, pride, guilt, and all other obstacles to peace. Christ nails them on His cross and buries them in His tomb. With them dead, we can relax into the abiding love of God and living in peace with Him and with all others.

"Do not be anxious about anything, but in everything, by prayer and petition, with thanksgiving, present your requests to God. And the peace of God, which transcends all understanding, will guard your hearts and your minds in Christ Jesus" (Philippians 4:6, 7).

NOTES

[1]Maisie Ward, *Gilbert Keith Chesterton.* Sheed & Ward, 1943, p. 232.
[2]*Blondie.* Copyright 1980 by King Features Syndicate, Inc.

HE PROMISES
A SPIRIT-FILLED LIFE

John 14:15-18, 25, 26; 16:12-15
Acts 2:38

How very hard it is to be
A Christian! Hard for you and me. . . .

—Robert Browning

Browning is not the only believer to complain of the high standard Christ sets for His followers. We know what we ought to do but find it nearly impossible to do it. We make Paul's lament our own:

"What I want to do I do not do, but what I hate I do. . . . For I have the desire to do what is good, but I cannot carry it out. For what I do is not the good I want to do; no, the evil I do not want to do—this I keep on doing" (Romans 7:15-19).

Sometimes we don't stop with self-criticism. "How can God expect so much of us?" we complain. "He knows we're only human. He made us this way, after all. It is unfair of Him to make us so weak but expect so much!"

Our complaints ignore one of Christ's greatest promises, the gift of the Holy Spirit. Jesus does not expect us to meet His expectations on our own strength. He promises instead that He himself will be at work in us.

We approach the subject of the Holy Spirit carefully, because so many promises—not all of them Biblical—are made about the Spirit today that the subject is one of the most confusing teachings in contemporary Christianity. Several years ago I ended my own confusion by forgetting all the conflicting claims I had heard and doing my own study. With the help of a good concordance I looked up every Scriptural reference to the Spirit. What I found gave me a new appreciation of the real work of the Spirit. I want to discuss three of the truths I discovered.

THE HOLY SPIRIT POINTS TO CHRIST

This is the first one: the Holy Spirit points to Christ. *"He will bring glory to me* by taking from what is mine and making it known to you," Jesus promises His disciples (John 16:14). A quick review of early church history shows the Spirit fulfilling Jesus' promise. His role in Acts is to pave the way for the preaching of Christ.

On the miraculous Day of Pentecost the Spirit descends in tongues as of fire with a roar like a violent wind, holding the attention of the great crowd so that Peter can preach his great sermon about Christ (Acts 2).

A little later Peter makes his bold defense before the Sanhedrin, after he and John have been jailed for healing a beggar and preaching Christ. When charged to defend himself and explain "by what power or what name" he has been acting, "Peter, *filled with the Holy Spirit,*" tells them about Jesus. The Spirit is pointing to Christ.

When Peter and John are released and have reported to their fellow disciples, "after they prayed, the place where they were meeting was shaken. And they were all *filled with the Holy Spirit* and spoke the word of God boldly." With the help of the Spirit they courageously preach Christ.

So it goes through the book of Acts. The Holy Spirit commands Philip to go to the chariot in which the Ethiopian eunuch is riding—so that Philip can tell the stranger about Christ (8:29).

Ananias tells Saul that the Lord has sent him to Saul "so that you may see again and *be filled with the Holy Spirit*" (9:17). The result of the Spirit's activity is Paul's lifetime spent in pointing to Christ.

These are enough instances to establish the fact that the Holy Spirit's work, as Jesus says, is to bring glory to Christ. The Spirit's task is not to call attention to himself. Christian preaching, therefore, does not concentrate on the Holy Spirit; instead, it lifts up the One whom the Spirit has come to glorify.

Charles Fuller, for many years the preacher of radio's Old Fashioned Revival Hour, was bothered by this subject early in his ministry. After preaching in his own church on Sunday mornings, he regularly visited Bethel Temple in the afternoon. Many members of this church claimed to speak in tongues. Fuller did not and he was bothered by what he thought must be an incompleteness in his Christian life. He spoke of his concern to the minister of Bethel, a Dr. Eldredge, who wisely counseled him, "Charlie, what you need to seek is the Giver, not the gifts."[1]

Christ is the Giver of gifts to the church (see Ephesians 4:11). We can become terribly distraught if we make the mistake of judging the depth of our spirituality by our possessing one or another of the gifts of Christ's Spirit. More than once, for example, well meaning but misguided Christian friends have questioned my own spiritual life because I do not speak in tongues. They made me feel ashamed that I was lacking something that they considered the mark of the Spirit's presence in my life. A Christian counselor comforted me with the knowledge that speaking in tongues is mentioned in only 3 of the 66 books of the Bible and in only 7 of its 1189 chapters. Can an activity that receives so little Scriptural attention be essential to being a disciple of Christ, especially since it is nowhere deemed necessary for salvation or even recommended for Christian growth?

We are presently caught up in the same atmosphere which Alexander Campbell decried in the nineteenth century: "In the present day we seem to have more of the religion of excitement, than we have of the excitement of religion."[2] There is no denying the excitement which the charismatic movement has brought to today's religious scene. In fact, I am grateful for the movement's contribution: we needed to be shaken and released from the shackles of cold rationalism and formal legalism. So I am not attacking the excitement which has resulted from this emphasis upon the Holy Spirit; I am merely warning us away from making a religion of the excitement or letting the Holy Spirit replace the Lord Jesus Christ as the center of Christian experience. The Spirit desires to call attention neither to himself nor to the individual Christian. His task is to turn our eyes upon Jesus.

THE HOLY SPIRIT BUILDS UP THE CHURCH—AND HELPS US TO DO OUR PART

Having stressed the importance of seeking the Giver and not the gifts, we can safely think together about the gifts. That the Holy Spirit endows disciples of Christ with an abundance of good gifts is so well known to Christians that little Scriptural documentation is needed. The only fact that is disputed is the purpose for the Spirit's gifts. The Bible is emphatic: the Lord gives His gifts to believers so they can do their part in building up the church. (See Ephesians 4 and 1 Corinthians 12—14.)

First, a word about Corinth. This troubled church was rocked with division. The members were disputing doctrinal issues, dividing in their loyalty to this or that preacher, winking at gross immorality, puzzling over Christian teachings regarding marriage and sexual behavior, and profaning the sacred observance of the Lord's Supper. Yet many of these same members were proud, even arrogant, because they could speak in tongues. They were turning corporate worship into chaos and destroying, rather than building up, the church. To correct these abuses, Paul sternly reprimands them one moment, lovingly chastises them another, and consistently exhorts them to walk a higher way.

Regarding the issue of tongues, which he tactfully discusses in chapters 12 through 14, his position leaves no doubt. He has the gift of tongues himself (1 Corinthians 14:18), but he considers it of minimal value (14:19), since it lacks the ability of "intelligible words to instruct others" and thus to edify fellow Christians.

In addition, he places tongues in the context of the many other gifts of the Spirit, which he lists (12:1-11) as

the message of wisdom [How often do you hear this gift praised?], the message of knowledge [Or this one?], faith, gifts of healing, miraculous powers, prophecy, ability to distinguish between spirits, ability to speak in different kinds of tongues, and interpretation of tongues.

Before listing these gifts, Paul insists to his Corinthian friends that each one of them "is given for the common good." Never is any gift of the Spirit given so that the recipient can call attention to or in any other way serve himself!

Paul offers another list of gifts in Romans 12:6-8. Here he includes prophesying, serving, teaching, encouraging, contributing to the needs of others, leadership, and showing mercy—certainly less exciting than tongues, but more useful in building up the body.

It is apparent from these lists that a *gift* is not necessarily the same as a *talent*. A difference is in the use that is made of it. You may sing beautifully, but if you sing for your own sake—either to promote your career or earn applause—it is merely a talent, not a gift. You may have fine managerial skills and be an effective leader, but if you benefit only yourself with it, you have talent but no spiritual gift. The Holy Spirit can make naturally talented persons real blessings to the church, their talent becoming His gift to the body. He can also take humbly endowed persons and, through His power, turn them into genuinely gifted ones through whom the church is blessed. This is His desire: to build Christ's church.

Acts reveals some characteristics of a Spirit-filled church. The Spirit wants it to be *honest.* When Ananias and Sapphira decided to join the rest of the disciples in selling their property and donating the sale price to the church to relieve the poor, they seemed to be doing a noble deed. It was only pretense, however, because they secretly agreed to withhold some of the money from the church. They had every right to keep as much of their money as they wanted to—but they had no right to lie. Peter asked Sapphira, "How could you agree to test the *Spirit* of the Lord? Look! The feet of the men who buried your husband are at the door, and they will carry you out also." They had sold, they had given—but they had lied. The Spirit wants an honest church! (Acts 5:9).

And a *mission-minded* church. While the Christians in Antioch "were worshiping the Lord and fasting, the Holy Spirit said, 'Set apart for me Barnabas and Saul for the work to which I have called them' " (13:2). The Spirit leads the church to love and want to save those who are not yet within the body.

The Spirit wants a *united* church. Because of the success of Paul and Barnabas, the Christian church faced its first severe crisis. The missionaries were admitting Gentiles as well as Jews into the church without requiring them to obey all the Law of Moses. Orthodox Jewish Christians could not believe that God would allow such heresy! To deal with the dispute, the elders at Jerusalem presided over a conference of the Jewish plaintiffs and the defendants, Paul and Barnabas and others from Antioch. Peter carried the day for unity when he addressed the assembly, "God, who knows the heart, showed that he accepted them (Gentiles) by giving *the Holy Spirit* to them, just as he did to us" (15:8). At the conclusion of the meeting a few instructions were sent to Antioch in the name of the unifying Spirit: "It seemed good to the Holy Spirit and to us not to burden you with anything beyond the following requirements . . ." (15:28). The Spirit desires a unified church.

"Since you are eager to have spiritual gifts," Paul has written, "try to excel in gifts that build up the church . . ." (1 Corinthians 14:12).

THE HOLY SPIRIT HELPS THE CHRISTIAN KNOW AND LIVE THE TRUTH

Even if we admit that the Spirit points to Christ and builds up the church, we still want to know, "What does the Spirit do for me?"

He does *not* do many things for which He is blamed. A Michigan man received a life sentence after beating his wife to death with a baseball bat and severely injuring two of his five children. He said he was saving his family from Satan. He had been reading his Bible for several hours before committing this atrocity. Did the Spirit tell him to do this?

A Mississippi man shot and killed his wife and six relatives because, he said, the Lord's voice ordered him to. What is the Spirit's voice?

Not every voice that we think is the Spirit's comes from Him! Not every act that we attribute to the Spirit is committed by Him! Not every warm religious feeling that we think is the Spirit moving in us is His! Jesus has not sent the Spirit to heat up our feelings or make us all miracle workers or to whisper sweetly in our ears.

To His disciples Jesus said that the Spirit will be a Counselor who tells us the Truth. He will remind the disciples of "everything I have said to you." Thus, when we read what these disciples have written about Jesus, the One to whom the Spirit points, the Spirit will also lead us to the truth of how His present disciples must live.

Remember Ananias' promise to Saul that he would be filled with the Spirit? Note the working of that Spirit in the rest of Paul's life. He was still subject to the usual physical limitations—he could not walk on water or appear and disappear at will. He was still harassed by his thorn in the flesh (2 Corinthians 12:7-10); he still suffered abuse from enemies. But through the power of the Spirit he could teach the truth about Jesus, serve His cause, stand up to His enemies, even love His enemies, and pioneer His mission. No one can doubt the Spirit was at work in Paul—to point to Christ, to build up Christ's church, and to help Paul know and live the truth.

Because he had his mind "set on what the Spirit desires" (Romans 8:5), Paul could accomplish marvels for Christ. As far as he was concerned, however, the Spirit's task is not to make miracle workers out of us but to build Christlike character in us. Until the Holy Spirit takes control of your life, you naturally lust for what is contrary to the Spirit. The results are painful to look at: "sexual immorality, impurity and debauchery; idolatry and witchcraft; hatred, discord, jealousy, fits of rage, selfish ambition, dissensions, factions and envy; drunkenness, orgies, and the like." (See Galatians 5:16-23.)

But when the Holy Spirit takes over, He produces Christlike character. The fruit of the Spirit's work in your life is "love, joy, peace, patience, kindness, goodness, faithfulness, gentleness and self-control."

What, then, could be better than Christ's promise of a Spirit-filled life?

NOTES

[1]Daniel P. Fuller, *The Story of Charles E. Fuller—Give the Winds a Mighty Voice.* Waco: Word Books, 1972, p. 36.

[2]Alexander Campbell, "The Religion of Excitement, and the Excitement of Religion." *Millennial Harbinger,* 1839, p. 34.

HE PROMISES
A CONSEQUENTIAL LIFE

Matthew 25

Cheer up! You have two chances—
One of getting the germ and one not.
And if you get the germ, you have
    two chances—
One of getting the disease and one not.
And if you get the disease, you have
    two chances—
One of dying and one of not.
And if you die—well, you still have
    two chances!

I found this little bit of nonsense years ago. Why I've kept it I'm not sure. Perhaps for its humor, although its subject is no laughing matter! Besides, it is wrong!

There is no *if* about dying. You will die—not whether but *when* is the question. Of course, we avoid thinking about it as much as possible. For most of us death is something that happens to other people. We are like American author William Saroyan, who called the Associated Press before his death to leave this statement: "Everybody has got to die, but I have always believed an exception would be made in my case. Now what?"[1]

You will die, that is certain. It is also certain that when you die, there will be nothing chancy about your destiny. You will get what you have prepared for.

You may already be protesting that this chapter is out of place in a book on the promises of Jesus. Let me defend myself. If His promises have any value at all, they are consequential. Christians are persons who have believed the promises of Jesus and are enjoying the consequences.

In Matthew 25 Jesus tells three stories which illustrate the long-term effects of everyday choices. Every story presupposes the value and importance of every human being. *You* are important: what *you* do, what *you* believe, and what *you* are matters. Even your little everyday acts resound with eternal overtones.

The parable of the ten virgins contrasts five wise maidens, who prepared for the bridegroom's arrival, with five foolish ones, who failed to think ahead. The five wise ones enjoyed the consequences; the five foolish did not.

In the parable of the talents two men managed their master's money well and enjoyed his praise. The third did nothing to increase the value of what his master had given him, so even what little he had been given was taken from him. The productive servants were rewarded with greater responsibilities; the unproductive one was cast out. All three bore the consequences of their decisions.

Jesus' picture of the Day of Judgment develops the same theme. The basis of the last judgment will be individual acts of kindness to the very needy. A cup of water given, a meal prepared, a visit to prison, a loving service to the sick—the seemingly insignificant acts will be remembered forever.

I recently attended Claudia Dietz's funeral. She had finally been released from her struggle against cancer. A gracious and humble minister's wife, she would never have anticipated the crowd that assembled for her funeral. People came from miles around to pay silent tribute to the woman whose influence was out of proportion to her worldly position. Those of us honoring her were not surprised, however; she had embodied the teachings of all three stories. She had prepared for her meeting with the Lord, she had wisely managed the talents God had given her, and she had faithfully cared for the hungry and sick and imprisoned. She had lived a consequential life!

CONSEQUENCES IN TIME

Jesus' stories do not draw a strict line between time and eternity, but let's do so for a moment. Think first of the results your decisions have on your life right now. You don't need to be reminded of the results of a smoking habit, or an imbalanced or gluttonous diet, or the abuse of drugs and alcohol. I am equally concerned about destructive emotions or the abuse of the mind through mental laziness or a diet of propaganda or pornography. It may take a few years, but sooner or later sins will reap their ruinous harvest.

That is painfully clear to me in middle age. I have concluded that the gravest threat to adult health is adolescence—our own! In those years we feel robust, confident, even immortal. So we are careless of body and character, oblivious to the price we will pay later for the sins of our youth. Somebody has said that old age loves to give advice since it no longer can set a bad example. Perhaps, but maybe it is the attempt of the too-late-wise to warn none-too-smart youth of the consequences.

We must also consider the effect we have on our loved ones. How often I think of these words from the Ten Commandments:

> "You shall not make for yourself an idol in the form of anything in heaven above or on the earth beneath or in the waters below. You shall not bow down to them or worship them; for I, the Lord your God, am a jealous God, punishing the children for the sin of the fathers *to the third and fourth generation* of those who hate me, but showing love to thousands who love me and keep my commandments" (Exodus 20:4-6).

If I had never read this Scripture, I would still have known its truth. Inevitably, when searching for some clue that will help me understand a troubled person, I ask, "What was your father like, or your mother?" The behavior of parents is incredibly important in the development of their children. As Shakespeare's Mark Antony said of Caesar, "The evil that men do lives after them. . . ." It often lives in their descendants.

When we consider our impact on the lives of others, we have to admit that no one who matters can live a strictly private life. Never can I say that what I do or think or am is only my own affair—unless I am important to no one else. Whenever someone says, "I can do whatever I want to, it is only my affair," he is confessing his low opinion of himself.

Jesus takes just the opposite point of view. He believes that *you* are important and *your* actions have consequences— for yourself (Matthew 25:1-13), for the Lord's work on earth (25:14-30), and for others whose suffering you could ease (25:31-46). It is no wonder Paul urges Christians "to live a life worthy of the calling you have received" (Ephesians 4:1), to recognize your importance, to be a person of beneficial consequences.

When teenagers go wrong, they do not do so because they

burn with desire to be sinful but because they do believe themselves to be unimportant. My wife and I have had to admit that our teenagers will do anything they want when we are not around. If we have brought them up in fear of us, they will rebel as soon as possible. But if we have convinced them that they are truly important individuals—important to us, to God, to themselves, and to their other loved ones—we will not have to worry about them.

The alcoholic who boasts, "I'm as strong as an ox; yes, I drink a lot, but I am not hurting anyone except myself," cannot really get away with this. When he is buried by his grey-haired father, his wife and three children, and a few friends, none will believe he hurt no one but himself.

The person who says, "I just don't want to bother God with my problem" does not know much about Him. God's message to mankind is that every human being is important to God—even this man! We are important enough for Him to send Christ for us, to establish a church for us, and to give us the Holy Spirit to help us. We sin because we do not think as highly of ourselves as God does. And we bear the consequences.

CONSEQUENCES IN ETERNITY

Jesus' stories move readily from time to eternity. Death is a pause on our journey from here to hereafter, with our later abode determined not so much by God's judgment as by our choice. A bridesmaid who is too careless to prepare for the wedding banquet has, in effect, chosen not to go. A servant who fears his Master and then excuses his poor stewardship by blaming the Master has really chosen to live away from the One he fears and hates. A person who so loves others that he takes responsibility to care for them will be invited to live in their presence in the kingdom of God forever.

Since time merges into eternity, how would you like for the way you are now living to go on forever? Let's put the question another way. We all have our dreams. Suppose, like some character on TV's *Fantasy Island,* you were granted your fantasy. Would it be good for you or not? If you could live your fantasy, would you want to live it forever?

I don't preach enough about judgment. Perhaps I am still reacting to my earlier years when I spoke too enthusiastically on the subject. I certainly never sounded like the preacher Charles R. Brown describes:

"My beloved hearers, if I may call you so, you are under some measure of moral obligation to repent, so to speak; and in case you do not, I would venture to suggest that there is a remote possibility that you may be damned as it were, to a certain extent."[2]

My sermons were more pointed; God's judgment was burningly real to me.

It still is, although further reading of the Scriptures has convinced me that God does not so much judge us as grant us our wishes. The message of repentance which the above preacher is trying so weakly to deliver is a vital one. It urges a turning toward God away from everything that tempts us away from Him. To repent is to resist the seductions of the flesh. It requires you to abandon the empty excuse that what you do doesn't matter. To turn toward God is to begin to think of yourself as God thinks of you, a person of infinite worth, designed to live in the court of the King forever.

To turn toward God is to learn that getting ready for Heaven is not as demanding as spiritual sluggards try to make it seem. In fact, as the poet Ben Jonson exclaimed, "Many might go to Heaven with half the labor they go to Hell." Heaven has to do with choosing God, with accepting His grace and forgiveness, with walking by faith in Him, with living as part of His family, with serving others in love, and with wanting to become like Jesus.

Preparing for Heaven is within everyone's reach. Even the one-talented man could have pleased his master—he was not *un*talented until he chose to hide his talent. Even the humblest person can give food to the hungry or clothes to the naked. Everyone can believe in the One God sent to save us!

Another famous Scripture teaches that the judgment is getting what you choose. We usually quote just part of it: "For God so loved the world that he gave his one and only Son, that whoever believes in him shall not perish but have eternal life" (John 3:16). There is no more comforting verse in the Bible. Rightly so, since it exposes the extent of God's love and His desire to save as many as possible. But the following sentences show the consequences of rejecting this promise:

Whoever believes in him is not condemned, but whoever

does not believe stands condemned already because he has not believed in the name of God's one and only Son. This is the verdict: Light has come into the world, but *men loved darkness instead of light because their deeds were evil* (John 3:18, 19).

In spite of God's offer of light, unbelievers *wanted* darkness, so they *chose* darkness—and they were given darkness, "where there will be weeping and gnashing of teeth" (Matthew 25:30).

For Jesus, Judgment Day is not so much a day of decision as the day on which the consequences of previous decisions will be made fully known. The person who has chosen to gain the whole world at the expense of his soul (Matthew 16:26) will be given what he wanted. He who has loved darkness rather than light will enter his chosen darkness. He who refuses to sing to his Creator will not be forced to join the chorus of God's angels. As Jesus has said elsewhere,

"As for the person who hears my words but does not keep them, I do not judge him. For I did not come to judge the world, but to save it. There is a judge for the one who rejects me and does not accept my words; that very word which I spoke will condemn him at the last day (John 12:47, 48).

He has spoken the truth. Those who desire the truth will hear and heed; those who prefer to ignore the truth will be granted their request. Jesus is the Way, the Truth and the Life; whoever chooses Him will have life abundant and eternal. It's a promise!

NOTES

[1]Quoted by Stan Mooneyhan, "Punctuating Life and Death." *World Vision,* August, 1981, p. 23.

[2]James W. Cox, "Pastor's Study." *Pulpit Digest,* November, December 1980, p. 7.

Textbooks
by Standard Publishing: